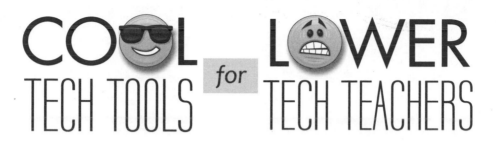

COOL LOWER
TECH TOOLS *for* TECH TEACHERS

COOL  LOWER *for* TECH TOOLS TECH TEACHERS

20 Tactics
for Every Classroom

William N. Bender ■ Laura B. Waller

CORWIN
A SAGE Company

CORWIN
A SAGE Company

FOR INFORMATION:

Corwin
A SAGE Company
2455 Teller Road
Thousand Oaks, California 91320
(800) 233-9936
www.corwin.com

SAGE Publications Ltd.
1 Oliver's Yard
55 City Road
London EC1Y 1SP
United Kingdom

SAGE Publications India Pvt. Ltd.
B 1/I 1 Mohan Cooperative Industrial Area
Mathura Road, New Delhi 110 044
India

SAGE Publications Asia-Pacific Pte. Ltd.
3 Church Street
#10-04 Samsung Hub
Singapore 049483

Printed in the United States of America

A catalog record of this book is available from the Library of Congress.

ISBN 978-1-4522-3553-0

Acquisitions Editor: Jessica Allan
Associate Editor: Julie Nemer
Editorial Assistant: Lisa Whitney
Production Editor: Cassandra Margaret Seibel
Copy Editor: Diane DiMura
Typesetter: C&M Digitals (P) Ltd.
Proofreader: Annie Lubinsky
Indexer: Rick Hurd
Cover Designer: Janet Kiesel
Permissions Editor: Karen Ehrmann

This book is printed on acid-free paper

SUSTAINABLE FORESTRY INITIATIVE
Certified Chain of Custody
Promoting Sustainable Forestry
www.sfiprogram.org
SFI-01268

SFI label applies to text stock

12 13 14 15 16 10 9 8 7 6 5 4 3 2 1

Contents

Acknowledgments

Corwin gratefully acknowledges the contributions of the following reviewers:

David Callaway
Seventh Grade Social Studies
   Teacher
Rocky Heights Middle School
Highlands Ranch, CO

Jolene Dockstader
Seventh Grade Language
   Arts Teacher
Jerome Joint School District
West Jerome, ID

Bena Kallick
Educational Consultant;
   Program Director,
   Eduplanet21
Westport, CT

Cheryl Oakes
Resource Room Teacher
Wells High School
Wells, ME

Rose Cherie Reissman
Literacy Specialist/
   Technology Integration
   Specialist
New York City Department of
   Education, IS 62
Brooklyn, NY

Chris Toy
Educational Consultant/
   Graduate School
   Instructor
Learning Capacity Unlimited/
   University of Southern
   Maine
Bath, ME

Barbara Trolley
Professor
Buffalo Center Counselor
   Education Program
   Director; Chair of the
   Disability Committee
St. Bonaventure University
   Buffalo Center
Hamburg, NY

About the Authors

William N. Bender is an international leader who focuses on practical instructional tactics with an emphasis on response to intervention (RTI) and differentiated instruction in general education classes across the grade levels. In particular, Dr. Bender has written more books on RTI than any other author in the world, two of which are best sellers. He has now completed seven books on various aspects of response to intervention, as well as a professional development videotape on that topic. He completes between 40 and 50 workshops yearly in the United States, Canada, and the Caribbean. In the fall of 2010, he was selected to work with the Ministry of Education in Bermuda to establish its nationwide RTI framework. One of his recent books, *Beyond the RTI Pyramid,* was a 2010 finalist for the Distinguished Achievement Award for Excellence in Educational Publishing.

Dr. Bender uses practical strategies and easy humor to make his workshops an enjoyable experience for all, and he is frequently asked to return to the same school or district for additional workshops. He consistently receives positive reviews of his professional-development workshops for educators across the grade levels. Dr. Bender believes his job is to inform educators of innovative, up-to-date tactics for the classroom, rooted in current research, in an enjoyable workshop experience. He is able to convey this information in a humorous, motivating fashion.

Dr. Bender began his education career teaching in a junior high school resource classroom, working with adolescents with behavioral disorders and learning disabilities. He earned his doctorate in special education from the University of North Carolina and has taught in leading universities around the nation, including Rutgers University and the University of Georgia. He is now consulting and writing full time and has published over 60 research articles and 23 books in education.

Laura B. Waller is an exciting, young, dynamic educator and the co-author of *RTI and Differentiated Reading in the K–8 Classroom* and *The Teaching Revolution: RTI, Technology, and Differentiation Transform Teaching for the 21st Century.* Ms. Waller began her career as a reading specialist in elementary education, working at an inner-city school in Washington, DC. With degrees from both Appalachian State University and Johns Hopkins University, she succeeded in her teaching of English-learning students, underprivileged students, Title I students, and many other students who struggled in reading and mathematics.

Ms. Waller is now teaching underprivileged children in a rural school in North Carolina and doing workshops for educators on technology for reading instruction and differentiated instruction in core academic areas. She also offers workshops on classroom use of Smart Boards, e- assessments, and other technologies to facilitate differentiation and academic progress. She recently received funding from the Bright Ideas Grant to implement hands-on literacy centers that support learning with a focus on technology and preparing students to be globally competitive in the 21st century. Her instructional practices have been featured in a professional development video, *Differentiating Math Instruction* (Corwin, 2009).

Introduction

We believe that this book may be the most important professional development book you will ever read! Further, we believe that virtually every teacher, worldwide, should have access to this book. While we admit that statement is perhaps a bit self-serving, it is a fact that the topics discussed here, the specific, step-by-step guidelines for using technology tools in the classroom, and the teaching tactics presented below are drastically changing teaching today (Bender & Waller, 2011). Further, almost all teachers realize that they must update themselves constantly within the pantheon of these ever-evolving tech tools, in order to remain relevant and effective in the classroom.

Not only are these tech tools facilitating better delivery of information, they are changing the very fabric of the teaching and learning process in a fundamental sense, as students become creative developers of information rather than merely passive consumers of information (Wilmarth, 2010). For that reason, if for no other, we believe that every teacher simply must join this technology revolution quickly. This book can help you do just that.

> Almost all teachers realize that they must update themselves constantly within the pantheon of these ever-evolving tech tools, in order to remain relevant and effective in the classroom.

This is a book for those who have been somewhat reluctant to embrace technology in teaching, a book for principals to give to their faculty members who have let other teachers take the lead in tech applications. This book will help make the transition into teaching with technology relatively painless, though we do not use the term *easy!* We have chosen to describe tech tools here that represent first steps into tech-based teaching and that can be implemented by an individual teacher, rather than more broadly based tech tools that are typically implemented by schools or school districts. For example, we have chosen not to describe an entire class of tech tools that are collectively referred to as "class management systems" (e.g., Moodle or Schoology). While those tools effectively combine many of the individual tech tools discussed herein, they are generally subscription service tools that involve entire school faculties rather than individual teachers who are just beginning their tech journey.

There will be some work involved here, but we believe that we can demonstrate that this is well worth the effort. We give four very specific, first-step recommendations below that can be implemented by any teacher who is currently using e-mail. As that statement indicates, this book is not for the techno-oriented on the faculty but for other, less tech-savvy teachers. As we point out below, there are many reasons that teachers haven't implemented technology in their classes, and in that sense, this book is for us all.

> Technology is in the process of drastically changing the teaching and learning process.

We should note that, as this book was written in 2012, many teachers found themselves struggling to keep up with the tech tools for teaching, tools that other teachers were using daily (Bender & Waller, 2011; Ferriter & Garry, 2010). Of course, by 2012, many schools had already undertaken the goal of making Internet-based learning a primary feature in each classroom. Some schools purchased laptops for all students, while other schools purchased less expensive iPads or other tablets (Pemberton, 2011). Today, schools that are not already wireless are struggling to become so, and almost all educators realize that tech-based instruction represents not only learning for the future, but a true, life-long learning option for today's students (Bender & Waller, 2011). For that reason, the National Educational Technology Standards issued by the International Society for Technology in Education (www.iste.org/standards.aspx) stresses technology applications for virtually all classrooms, and the Common Core State Standards that have been adopted by forty-six states (as of 2012) likewise include a heavy emphasis on 21st century technology throughout the instructional process.

Each week seems to bring new announcements about a new tech tool for education. For example, the Apple Computer Company announced in January of 2012 that they were partnering with several textbook publishers to foster production of e-book textbooks, and that innovation alone promises to drastically change education within the next five years. The advent of social networking is also influencing classrooms around the world as teachers seek ways to use the modern mobile networking technologies such as Facebook or Twitter for teaching. These tech tools are causing a true revolution in instruction, and most of these tools didn't even exist five years ago (Pemberton, 2011; Richardson, 2010; Winn, 2012).

Isn't Everyone a Lower-Tech Teacher?

While this book has been developed with "lower-tech" teachers in mind, there are tactics and teaching ideas presented herein that will appeal to many current technology-oriented teachers as well. In fact, technology is evolving so fast that virtually all teachers can benefit from ideas on interesting technology applications. In some sense, virtually everyone in education today may be considered a lower-tech teacher! One would have to work virtually full time in order to implement, or even remain cognizant of, all of the tech tools for instruction out there! While almost all teachers are technology savvy to some degree, many freely acknowledge that they are not as current in using these quickly developing tech tools as they could be. Of course, one reason for this is obvious; if a school does not have Internet or widespread wifi capability, there has been little reason for teachers to begin using these emerging tech tools for teaching. In short, the infrastructure in many schools has not been sufficient to support these tech-based instructional innovations. How can one assign computer work when computers are not available in the classroom for each student? How can one assign research on the Internet when connectivity is not yet available? How can a teacher use a webquest, a wiki, or cloud-based educational services (all of which are described below) when students do not have access?

In fact, many teachers today are lower-tech, not because they don't use these modern tech tools, but because of the limited availability of them in the school. We have discussed this very issue with many teachers who freely admit that they use fewer tech tools in their teaching than they do in their personal lives! Many teachers use e-mail, Facebook, a blog, or a Twitter account, but they have not had a good opportunity to apply these tech tools in the classroom because of limited

> If a school does not have wifi capability, there has been little reason for teachers to move into using many of these emerging tech tools.

wifi or limited computer availability for students. Thus, many teachers have not yet explored the use of tech innovations, some of which have been around since the mid-1990s!

A recent national survey indicated that teachers wanted access to more technology in their classes (Quillen, 2012). In fact, even teachers who had some access to computers in their own class indicated a desire for increased technology options to meet the instructional needs of their students. In that sense, many teachers are lower-tech teachers and have not yet explored the rich instructional options that modern tech tools can provide.

To illustrate this point, the senior author of this book asked about the use of webquests among faculties from three different schools at three different workshops in the fall of 2011. Webquest is a tech tool that has been around since 1995 and is frequently used in many classrooms. However, we found that many teachers have never even used that instructional tactic. Faculty size among the three schools averaged fifty-five teachers, and in each case between two and four teachers indicated that they *had* done a webquest with their students. This admittedly unscientific information suggests that around 8 percent of these teachers were using this tech tool in their instruction, though virtually all of these teachers used e-mail in their communications with other faculty, administrators, and parents.

While a number of excellent professional development books on tech-based instruction are available, the vast majority of these books are written for cutting-edge, tech-savvy teachers—teachers that live and breathe technology!

One teacher who had used this tech tool found it necessary to reserve the computer lab at her school for that activity. She then had to move her class to that location, while displacing the computer teacher and the computer lab class for that period! It is easy to understand why many teachers have not tried these exciting teaching tools as yet.

However, there is yet another problem for teachers who want to use these tech tools in their instruction—the use of tech jargon that only tech-savvy teachers might understand. Further, much of the professional development literature on tech tools is likewise overly dependent on such jargon, and this leaves lower-tech teachers out in the cold. Terms such as *Web 2.0*, *social networking*, and *wikis* are unknown to some teachers in situations in which web access has been limited.

Further, while a number of excellent professional development books on tech-based instruction are available, the vast majority of these books are written for cutting-edge, tech-savvy teachers—teachers that live and breathe technology! These books are not generally intended for the lower-tech teachers who are just beginning to use these tech tools, and the jargon itself becomes a barrier to tech-based teaching.

This book is intended, not for the tech-savvy teacher who has widely explored any and all tech-based instructional options, but for the lower-tech teachers, almost all of whom use technology daily in their personal lives and realize they must soon begin to teach with these tech tools. We wanted to develop a more helpful book that carefully explained the jargon and the tech-teaching issues, specifically for these lower-tech teachers. To put the matter simply, that's exactly where most teachers are on tech-tool implementation in the classroom. This book is intended as a practical, useful guide for them. In short, if a teacher can do e-mail, he or she can implement many, if not all, of the tech tools discussed here.

> This book is intended, not for the tech-savvy teacher who has widely explored any and all tech-based instructional options, but for the lower-tech teachers, almost all of whom use technology daily in their personal lives and realize they must begin to explore these instructional options.

What If Our School Can't Do It Yet?

My school doesn't have wifi in my class yet!

We have wifi, but I don't have the computers I need to put my whole class online!

I've decided to let the teacher in the computer lab handle that!

We've heard all of these comments and more on why teachers have not moved into tech-tool teaching. First of all, we want to note that it is certainly reasonable of teachers to note the problems resulting from limited wifi or limited Internet capable devices. Further, it is also fair to point out that the vast majority of students are learning in most classrooms without using these newly emerging tech tools. Given these realities, teachers might wonder, "What if our school can't do this yet? What can I do?"

Here are several points to consider. First, on the availability of wifi, schools across the United States are rushing to upgrade wifi availability throughout the building. In contrast, Canadian teachers often report that their schools are somewhat ahead of schools in the United States in terms of access to the web. Of course, concerns related to limited Internet access are likely to decrease each year, as more schools prepare themselves for wifi capability. However, even without wifi, teachers have some options for using these tech tools. Moving to a classroom where wifi and computers are available is one option, though admittedly a cumbersome option, as discussed above. However, we've run into some other, more creative solutions that teachers themselves have generated. One teacher used her own smartphone as a mobile "hotspot." Some smartphones can serve as a wifi hub for up to five computers or iPads, and depending on the data plan that a teacher has, this might involve little or no additional cost. This might be an option to consider for occasional tech-tool use, at least until wifi is available schoolwide. It is also possible for individual schools to build several such wifi capable phones into the budget and share them among teachers.

Another option for using these tech tools involves the simple idea of giving students more time on tech-based assignments. Some teachers are making webquest, wiki, or other tech-tool assignments merely by giving the assignment and allowing several days to complete the work. Students can then access the required technology in the computer lab at school between classes, in the school media center, at a local library, at home, or simply by using a relative's smartphone.

We discussed this very idea with one teacher whose class had neither computers nor wifi capability. She used this "multiple-days" option by requiring students to access computers elsewhere to complete their work and then e-mailing the assignment to her. When asked why she did that, she gave a thought-provoking and compelling answer—"I cannot let the school's wifi limitations limit the future of my kids!" That answer is telling. Why indeed should teachers let school limitations negatively impact their instruction and the future learning options for their students?

Another option that many schools across the nation have initiated is the BYOD option: Bring Your Own Device! Schools simply request that students bring a wifi capable device to school with them, and then schools supplement those devices with some additional laptops or tablets in the classroom as the school budgets allow. Schools that have initiated this are witnessing dramatic increases in student engagement and academic achievement when they merely encourage students to bring their own device for Internet access (Wagner, 2011; Winn, 2012). In these cases, anything from a smart phone to a laptop will do, and when assignments are made in class, students can "double up" and share the devices that are available.

> "I cannot let the school's wifi limitations limit the future of my kids!"

In short, we would like to both honor and recommend the position stated so clearly by the teacher above—*Don't let school limitations limit learning for your students.*

Why Should I Implement Technology Now?

Given the time-crunch realities that teachers face daily—the need for more planning time, hours and hours of grading students' work, and so on, some teachers may still wonder, "Why should I implement this stuff? We do have a computer lab or a required computer class, so why should I make that effort in my science, history, or health class?"

The basic answer is simple; students learn demonstrably better when modern tech tools are used regularly and are well integrated throughout the curriculum. Evidence has indicated that tech tools increase students' engagement with the content, their excitement about learning, and ultimately their academic achievement (Barseghian, 2011; Cook, 2011; Keim, 2012). While much of the evidence is anecdotal in nature, the evidence is mounting that these tech tools work.

We strongly recommend that every educator view a 2010 PBS show called "Digital Nation" (Dretzen, 2010; available online from the PBS show *Frontline* at www.pbs.org/wgbh/pages/frontline/digitalnation/view). In that video, Principal Jason Levy, the administrator of a troubled school in the South Bronx of New York City, reported that laptops helped his students tremendously. Attendance went up, school violence went down, and reading and math achievement both increased (30 percent and 40 percent respectively) once students were provided with laptops and teachers integrated them into their instruction. While other research has not shown such impressive results resulting from use of these tech tools, the bulk of the evidence does suggest impressive achievement gains when tech tools are well integrated into the curriculum (Bender & Waller, 2011; Keim, 2012).

However, the *well-integrated* phrase in that conclusion is critical. Merely having computers or iPads in the classroom is not enough to increase achievement. These tech tools and the instructional methods they facilitate must be well integrated into the class; they must be used as fundamental components of the class on a regular basis in order to positively impact students' lives. Of course, that application of these tech tools usually requires and demands the informed judgment of a qualified teacher. In short, the teacher is still the most important single factor in student learning, and it is up to the teacher to integrate these tech tools into the curriculum in a meaningful fashion, in order to get the impressive achievement gains noted above.

It is clear that modern technologies are drastically changing the world in which today's students live, and this will inevitably impact every teacher's class (Bender & Waller, 2011; Wilmarth, 2010; Winn, 2012). Still, it is very easy to be overwhelmed by the vast array of instructional technologies today because new tech tools are evolving so quickly. This book is intended to erase that sense, and make the move into tech-tool teaching a bit gentler. Still, one thing is clear; our world is fast segregating itself into those that use these technologies daily for learning and those that don't. This is often referred to as the *digital divide*, and no educator would wish to condemn students to a life on the wrong side of that divide.

> Students learn demonstrably better when modern tech tools are used and are well integrated throughout the curriculum.

To further emphasize how important the use of these technologies are in education, one need only consider that the nation of India, in October of 2011, developed a tablet (somewhat comparable to the early iPads) that can be sold to the general public for the equivalent of $39! What happens economically in our world if every student in the nation of India, the second most populous nation on the planet, becomes educated completely within the digital world, while many students in the United States and other nations are not? Who then, will be on the wrong side of the digital divide?

It is now an iron-clad certainty that students of the 21st century will be using all of these tech tools to interact with their world, and educators would be remiss if we do not provide instruction within this tech-tool framework. To put the matter simply, teachers must embrace these modern tech tools for teaching in order to provide the best possible instruction for our students. Choosing not to do so is no longer an option, and the good news is that almost all teachers realize this.

Today, teachers are rushing to prepare themselves with these tools. Many schools are already using digital media and social networking sites to join the world of their students, and this tends to make the curriculum both more relevant and much more interesting to 21st century students (Rapp, 2009). While research on application of these tech tools is briefly summarized in many sections of this book, research is not the primary focus here. Rather, practical application tips and step-by-step guidelines for specific tech tools are the main focus. Again, we owe our students the best instruction we can provide for the world in which they will be living two, three, or four decades from now. The only way we can do that is by embracing the use of one or several of these tools immediately, and then moving into others as our comfort level grows. This book provides enough tactics such that it will help both lower-tech and tech-savvy teachers do just that.

C2S2 Kids and Their Learning Expectations

One additional answer to the question, "Why should I do this?" is critical for teachers to understand; students learn differently today than previously. In fact, many experts have recognized these different learning strategies and student expectations, differences that have become prominent only within the last decade (Barseghian, 2012; Bender & Waller, 2011, Richardson, 2012; Waters, 2011). Each of these fundamental differences is related to the ongoing technology revolution. Here are four major learner characteristics of kids today:

- Students today learn differently and thrive in collaborative learning.
- Students today create content rather than consume content.
- Students today choose to invest significant time in a virtual, digital social environment.
- Students today are self-directed in that they wish to choose what to study, they want the option to learn on their own, and they absolutely insist on using technology in their learning.

As a form of shorthand for this changing learner, we use the concept *C2S2*, an acronym that stands for the four major characteristics of (some might say requirements from) today's learner.

C2S2 Kids are:

collaborative,
creative,
social, and
self-directed.

Once teachers understand these four basics about the changing learners today, educators can begin to get a more substantive handle on how teaching is changing. We have highlighted these points and these will form the basis of much of the discussion of various tech tools in the book, but the importance of these new student learning modes cannot be overstated. C2S2 kids really do learn differently and have different expectations of the learning environment.

First, students have demonstrated by their participation in social networking sites that they crave social, collaborative learning opportunities. A variety of tools have been presented herein to help use that desire for collaborative work as an educational motivational tool, and teachers must seize this amazing opportunity to increase the engagement of students with the content to be mastered. Should we miss that opportunity, we assure our own irrelevance in the eyes of our students. Further, in the workplace of the 21st century, collaborative skills oriented around specific tasks will be the defining element, and our classrooms today must reflect that.

Next, students are creating content today, rather than merely consuming information (Bender & Waller, 2011). In that sense, the 19th century model of instruction (i.e., students come into classrooms where teachers pour knowledge into their heads, which students then regurgitate on memory-based assessments) has given way to opportunities for students to create information and solve real-world problems. The creativity of millions and millions of students worldwide represents a vast, wholly untapped resource of thought that can now be directed at fundamental, real-world problems. In fact, that is the very basis of project-based learning, focusing students' collaborative creativity on real problems to seek real solutions that can then be applied in the real world (Bender & Waller, 2011).

Students today are creators and publishers of information (Waters, 2011), and in some cases that student-generated information can become important information for future students to review. Further, the growing emphasis on tech tools in the context of project-based learning focuses directly on students using modern technologies while solving relevant questions that they find highly motivational and addressing real-world problems and issues (Bender & Waller, 2011). Today, and for the future, students create content rather than merely consume content; one can only stand in awe of what the creative capacity of millions upon millions of students might bring, but lest we forget how creative young kids might be, we must remember that both Microsoft and Apple were essentially created by a group of "kids working in their garage"!

Next, teachers should understand that the social expectations of today's learners go far beyond collaborative work in the classroom. Even when students are not collaboratively working on a task, they crave today the opportunity to socially engage in discussions of their learning.

Students spend nearly unimaginable amounts of time in the digital, social environments of Facebook, Twitter, and many other social networks, and this desire for virtually unlim-ited social interaction can and should be harnessed as a powerful educational force. Teachers today simply must begin to use this force in order to reach our students.

Finally, students today are self-directed, and that inde-pendence is shown in at least three ways. First, they are demonstrating by their very actions that they wish to exer-cise some choice in what and when they study, and they wish to employ technology in vir-tually all aspects of their lives (Barseghian, 2012). There may be a brewing conflict herein. Today, educators seem increas-

> The growing emphasis on tech tools in the context of project-based learning focuses directly on students using modern technologies while solving relevant questions that they find highly motivational and addressing real-world problems and issues.

ingly inclined on setting rigorous curricular standards, such as the Common Core State Standards or even technology standards for informational literacy, while at the same time that students are self-directing what content they learn in their webquests, projects, and other classroom activities. While it is too early to tell, this may result in conflict, and we have begun to suspect that the setting of curricular standards beyond the broadest content guidelines might repre-sent a 20th century attempt to guide 21st century education.

Second, many students seem to thrive when presented with the oppor-tunity to study new content independently. The speed with which Khan Academy (see Tech Tool 6) has taken hold of education and the high levels of learning of many students using that tool—students going far beyond their own grade level in mathematics or other subjects—suggest that self-directed learning may be critical in the future of education. Educators should anticipate an explosion of open-source programs such as this, in an array of subject areas, within the next few years, and we would do well to implement these free programs. More so than any other tech tool, these can unleash the learning power of students worldwide.

Third, students are self-directed today, in the sense that they absolutely demand the use of technology in the classroom. According to Waters (2011), students from a number of schools in lower-income neighborhoods showed up at a recent meeting on technology in education demanding access to the same technology options as students from more affluent schools (Barseghian, 2012)! They held up cell phones and pointed out the lack of technology in their own schools. Barseghian (2012) provided a couple of quotes from students at that meeting that are quite telling:

> *How are we supposed to use technology responsibly if we don't use it at all?*

> *We're going to use technology to start a revolution, to improve our lives, and the lives of the upcoming generations, to get our voices heard.*

> *I demand that my peers and inner city school kids have a fair chance at life, furthering their education like privileged communities. Give us the resources we need. Because there are children like me who do give a damn about our future.*

Wow! Wisdom from the mouths of babes! Is there any educator alive who would not wish to respond to this reasonable, justifiable student demand for technology in our classrooms today? This book is intended as a nonthreatening effort to help teachers respond to these new student expectations! We intend to lead you, step-by-step, in this exciting process.

How Is This Book Organized to Help Me?

While literally hundreds of tech tools could have been included in this book, our intention is to make the transition to tech-based teaching a bit easier and more understandable for teachers. With that in mind, we'd like to describe the organization of this book and, in that context, make some suggestions on how teachers might use this book. First of all, the first four tech tools (web access, webquests, blogs, and wikis) are, in our view, essential in the classroom today, and we recommend that each teacher read those sections and implement those ideas. After teachers experiment with those tools for some time, they may wish to skip around a bit and explore various areas. Each of the twenty tools is defined at the outset, so teachers can quickly get an at-a-glance look at what a specific tech tool or application does, and if that is not of interest, teachers should skip it and select something they may find more useful given their subject area. Also, there are several more explicit suggestions for using these tools in the final section of the book, and we do urge all teachers to read that last section.

The tech tools are grouped into general sections, based on what we believe to be their main function in the classroom. The "basic four" tools we mentioned above are presented first in this book. Next, we present a series of six tech tools (Tech Tools 5 through 10) that facilitate increased student engagement with the subject content, and thereby foster anytime, anywhere learning. These tools will tend to make study topics more engaging and thereby increase student achievement.

Next, we present a series of eight tech tools (Tech Tools 11 through 18) to foster students' creativity, including tools that help students develop their work collaborative, and subsequently publish their work to an audience that is much wider than merely their own classroom. Finally, we present two tech tools (Tech Tools 19 and 20) that facilitate social networking and the formation of learning networks among students. Of course, in many discussions of specific tech tools we identify and briefly describe similar tech tools, even though those additional tools are not described thoroughly. In that sense, teachers can use this book and glean insight into many more than twenty tech tools. Here is a schematic of the overall organization.

Four Tools to Start With

> Tech Tool 1—Web Access, Laptops, and Mobile Devices
> Tech Tool 2—Webquests
> Tech Tool 3—Blogs
> Tech Tool 4—Wikis

Tools for Student Engagement and Empowerment

> Tech Tool 5—Cloud Computing
> Tech Tool 6—The Flipped Classroom and Khan Academy
> Tech Tool 7—Wiffiti
> Tech Tool 8—Jing
> Tech Tool 9—Gaming, ARGs, and Virtual World Instruction
> Tech Tool 10—Diigo

Tech Tools for Student Creation and Collaboration

> Tech Tool 11—Glogs
> Tech Tool 12—Podcasts
> Tech Tool 13—Scribd
> Tech Tool 14—Comic Life
> Tech Tool 15—Google Apps
> Tech Tool 16—Vokis, Avatars, and Animation!
> Tech Tool 17—Vlogs
> Tech Tool 18—Animoto

Tools for Social Learning and Networking

> Tech Tool 19—Facebook
> Tech Tool 20—Twitter

The Teaching Revolution and a Brave New World for the 21st Century

Finally, the list above shows how, in our opinion, these twenty tech tools may be best understood, and how they are generally related to each other. However, we must point out that many of these tools have multiple application options, and for that reason, many of these tools could have been placed in more than one of these book sections. Again, after the introduction and the first four tech tools, teachers are encouraged to skip around and find the tools that they are most interested in.

Small Steps Begin Epic Journeys

Begin Today!

We've all heard the adage that epic journeys begin with small steps, and that is absolutely true as teachers move into using tech tools in the classroom. This book walks teachers through their initial "small steps" in using tech tools in the classroom. For teachers that are beginning this journey, we recommend three specific tech tools in the next section that have been around for a while. For other, more tech-savvy teachers, we present some of the more recent, more innovative tech tools later in the book. Teachers should feel free to skip around, selecting the tools they would like to try.

Learn the Lingo

As in many new learning endeavors, the jargon, or specific language that is often associated with new things, can become a barrier, and that is as true in technology implementation as in any example we can think of. One illustration of that is the common use of the term *Web 2.0*. The term itself suggests that the web has been somehow redesigned for a new set of teaching applications, but nothing could be further from the truth. Web 2.0 refers to the usage of Internet sites rather than a second generation of redesigned websites. Web 2.0 is a loosely defined term that indicates the use of website for interactive collaboration between students, rather than merely as sites from which students can passively obtain content information. The first several tech tools described below illustrate this concept nicely. As described in the following sections, webquests typically involve students using websites to obtain information for research purposes, whereas wikis facilitate the option of having students collaborate to create information for use by others in the class. In that sense, the wiki would be an example of a Web 2.0 tech tool, and this book will present many others.

Start Small!

We strongly suggest that teachers explore only a few of these tools initially. Teachers should try each tool two or three times in their instructional units, taking several weeks to get used to using them. We do recommend the first four tools for almost all teachers initially, and teachers might begin with those. However, if one of those tools doesn't seem to work for your students, or you are not comfortable with it, then drop it and try another. No teacher should try all of these at once, and typically you will find it

> Web 2.0 is a loosely defined term that indicates the use of website for interactive collaboration between students, rather than merely as sites from which students can passively obtain content information.

much easier to start small! However, every teacher should realize that the application of even two or three of these tech tools will demonstrate the instructional relevance of your subject to the students in your class. In short, using two or three of these tech tools makes you a tech-savvy teacher!

Partner Up!

Of course, exploring tech tools that someone else in your school is already using is always a good idea, since that other teacher can guide you as you begin to teach with these tools. If you can find a teacher experienced with the tool you select, invite a partnership with that teacher focused on application of that particular tech tool. Also, check with your school district to see which of these tech tools may be supported by the tech person at the school or district level. Your media center person is also an excellent source for help and suggestions.

Review the Acceptable Use Policy on the Internet

Most schools today (but not all) have a policy on Internet usage by students, typically referred to as an acceptable use policy. Such policies are designed to protect the students, since the Internet itself is wholly ungoverned. Thus these often come in the form of a letter to the parents, describing how the Internet will be accessed, and discussing what the school will recommend as acceptable Internet use for the students. These policies may be either informative (merely informing parents of Internet usage at the school), or they might require a parent's signature.

In addition, many schools couple these policies with firewalls that specifically block the use of certain websites at the school. In fact, some schools have dated Internet firewalls and policies that block some websites that are now specifically recommended for instruction. For example, various schools have blocked social networking sites such as Facebook and Twitter, even though these can be used as effective modern teaching tools. Of course, these acceptable use policies should discourage social networking between students and teachers, but the recent instructional recommendations for using these networking sites focus on appropriate educational discussions that might be undertaken in this context (e.g., a Facebook page dedicated exclusively to US history, and managed by the history teacher). In those cases, it is now recognized as very appropriate to use social networking sites.

While firewall decisions are typically made by a technology person at the district office, teachers must occasionally take responsibility to assure that administrators and parents are informed about Internet usage. In some schools, parents have already been informed that students will be accessing appropriate Internet sites for educational purposes, perhaps via a paragraph in the student handbook, or a letter on videotaping at school and Internet usage, that is sent to all parents each year from the principal's office. If your school does not have such an appropriate use policy, we recommend that you check with your principal, and then inform parents of your intention to have students online via a simple letter describing appropriate usage.

> We recommend placing responsibility for appropriate Internet usage squarely on the students' shoulders, with extensive teacher oversight.

Further, we recommend placing responsibility for appropriate Internet usage squarely on the students' shoulders, with extensive teacher oversight. We recommend this procedure, since such personal responsibility policies usually result in teachers spending some time teaching students a few simple rules about Internet usage. The acceptable use policy letter at the end of this section can provide you with some guidance concerning Acceptable Use Policies. If teachers use such a letter, they should have both students and parents sign the letter, and then review the letter several times with their students, stressing the guidelines for appropriate Internet usage.

Begin Social Networking!

We do urge teachers, at a minimum, to establish some type of social networking (e.g., Facebook page or Twitter account) for two reasons. First, participation in the digital world (e.g., a Facebook page focused on your class content) will immediately impress your students with your overall relevance. Second, social networking offers many options for important professional development for teachers, as teachers can follow other educators online, picking up teaching tips, or ideas, or notes on articles they may wish to read on various teaching strategies. Such social networking takes virtually no time at all, and it will enrich your teaching! In fact, we usually begin technology workshops for low-tech teachers by having teachers set up a Twitter account.

If you would like, you can use a Twitter account and begin to follow us online (@williambender1). If you choose to do that, we'll be sending you a short message two or three times each week on educational matters, notes on brief articles on teaching that you might want to access, or teaching ideas for you to try. More on that idea is presented in the social networking sections later in this book (see Tech Tools 19 and 20).

Enjoy the Journey!

Finally, do enjoy this journey into the modern world of tech-tool teaching. You should begin the process knowing that your teaching will be impacted in many positive ways. As we indicated above, even limited wifi or limited computers in the class are merely obstacles that can be overcome, and teachers should not wait for schools to become equipped with more laptops, iPads, or wifi availability. By beginning now, you will find your enjoyment of teaching increase, along with the engagement of your students.

In fact, one important payoff for beginning to use these tech tools is your enjoyment of teaching. Even veteran teachers with many years in the classroom—teachers who may be less familiar with these tech tools— typically find that they and their students enjoy these innovative teaching ideas. We've had teachers tell us that these tech tools made the classroom really fun again, for both them and their C2S2 students! Thus, our invitation to you: Join the excitement today! Enjoy the tech-tools journey!

References

Barseghian, T. (2011). *Proof in study: Math app improves test scores (and engagement).* Retrieved from http://mindshift.kqed.org/2011/12//proof-in-study-math-app-improves-test-scores-and-engagement

Barseghian, T. (2012). *Students demand right to technology in schools.* Retrieved from http://www.pbs.org/mediashift/2012/03/students-demand-right-to-technology-in-schools074.html

Bender, W. N., & Waller, L. (2011). *The teaching revolution: RTI, technology, and differentiation transform teaching for the 21st century.* Thousand Oaks, CA: Corwin.

Cook, G. (2011). *A compelling way to teach math—"flipping" the classroom.* Retrieved from http://articles.boston.com/2011/09/18/bostonglobe/30172469_1_math-khan-academy-high-tech-education

Dretzen, R. (Director), & Rushkoff, D. (Writer). (2010, February 8). Digital Nation [Television series episode]. In R. Dretzen [Producer], *Frontline.* Boston, MA: WGBH/Public Broadcasting Service (PBS). Available at www.pbs.org/wgbh/pages/frontline

Ferriter, W. M., & Garry, A. (2010). *Teaching the iGeneration: 5 easy ways to introduce essential skills with web 2.0 tools.* Bloomington, IN: Solution Tree Press.

Keim, B. (2012). *iPad textbooks: Reality less revolutionary than hardware.* Retrieved from http://www.wired.com/wiredscience/2012/10/ipad-textbooks-learning

Pemberton, L. (2011, December 18). With iPads, Olympia students have world at their fingertips. *The Olympian.* Retrieved from http://www.theolympian.com/2011/12/18/1918639/with-ipads-olympia-students-have.html#storylink-cpy

Quillen, I. (2012). The right level of ed-tech access? Retrieved from http://blogs.edweek.org/edweek/DigitalEducation/2012/01/the_right_level_of_ed-tech_acc.html

Rapp, D. (2009, January). Lift the cell phone ban. *Scholastic Administrator.* Retrieved from http://www2.scholastic.com/browse/article.jsp?id=3751073

Richardson, W. (2010). *Blogs, wikis, podcasts, and other powerful tools for educators.* Thousand Oaks, CA: Corwin.

Richardson, W. (2012). Preparing students to learn without us. *Educational Leadership, 69*(5), 22–26. Retrieved from http://www.ascd.org/publications/educationa-leadership/feb12/vol69/num05/Preparing-Students-to-Learn-Without-Us.aspx

Wagner, R. (2011). *BYOT pilot program wildly successful at Sullivan South.* Retrieved from http://www.timesnews.net/article/9038798/byot-pilot-program-wildly-successful-at-sullivan-south

Waters, J. (2011, December 13). Broadband, social networking, and mobility have spawned a new kind of learner. *The Journal.* Retrieved from http://thejournal.com/Articles/2011/12/13/Broadband-Social-Networks-and-Mobility.aspx?Page=1

Wilmarth, S. (2010). Five socio-technology trends that change everything in teaching and learning. In H. H. Jacobs, *Curriculum 21: Essential education for a changing world.* Alexandria, VA: ASCD.

Winn, M. (2012). *Weatherford school district's Bring Your Own Device Technology initiative getting positive results.* Retrieved from http://www.star-telegram.com/2012/01/08/3643863/weatherford-school-districts-bring.html#storylink=cpy

Example

An Acceptable Use Policy for the Internet

Your School Name
100 Main St.
Somewhere, Somestate, USA

Date: September 1

Dear (parent's name):

I am excited to be working with your child in my class this year, and I wanted to let you know that we will be using several of the modern instructional tools available on the Internet. Under my guidance in class, it will be your child's responsibility to use the Internet appropriately in order to ensure safe use of this instructional tool. I wanted to inform you of this and recommend the following guidelines for your child's Internet use at home. These will be the guidelines used in my class at the school, and I will teach these to all of the students. Also, I have a poster of these guidelines posted in my room.

Acceptable Use of the Internet

- The Internet is a great tool for learning, but it is totally ungoverned. Therefore, you must use these rules to take responsibility for your own safety in using the Internet appropriately. Here are some general guidelines, and if you have any questions about any location on the Internet, talk with your teacher or your parents and, if appropriate, investigate that location together.
- You should access only informational websites where it is clear who is responsible for the website. It is your responsibility to evaluate the quality of information you get from the Internet, and your teachers will teach you how to do so.
- Never type in your name, your address, your phone number, your picture, your e-mail, the name of your school, or any other personal information that can be used to identify you, unless specifically instructed to do so by your teacher. It will be acceptable, under the teacher's guidance, to type in some of this information on private or "class only" Internet locations such as class blogs, or class wikis.
- If you see sexual content of any sort, or inappropriate language (cursing) used on a website, you should immediately leave that website and report it to your teacher.
- If anyone contacts you via the Internet or e-mail that you do not know personally, you are required to immediately make your teacher aware of that contact.
- Never post pictures of yourself or anyone else, unless the teacher recommends and approves of those pictures in advance. Such approval will typically be granted only for pictures of students completing class projects, and/or field trips.
- Never use the Internet or e-mail or any other digital communication to criticize or embarrass others, either students or teachers. That can be considered bullying, and bullying in any form is not tolerated at our school.

Again, I am looking forward to teaching your child this year. Please let me know if you have any questions on this policy or anything else in my class. I look forward to working with you.

Yours,
Your Name Here

Part I

Four Tools to Start With

Tech Tool 1

Web Access, Laptops, and Mobile Devices

What Do I Need to Know?

Virtually all educational experts agree that tech-based learning is the key to future learning and ultimately to work productivity, and web access is the most critical single tool in this transition. Web access is typically taken to mean students' ability to access the Internet at any point during the lesson in order to take advantage of the array of available educational resources.

> **Definition:** Web access is typically taken to mean students' ability to access the Internet at any point during the lesson in order to take advantage of the array of available educational resources.

However, access alone, that is, merely making wifi or hard-wired Internet options and laptop (or other) computers available, is not going to result in the phenomenal increase in learning that is promised by the tech revolution (Bender & Waller, 2011). In short, we now know that *the box is not enough!* Merely providing students with a computer or tablet (the box) and assuming that learning will take place is naïve, and ultimately counterproductive. Rather web access, coupled with computers or mobile devices, must be integrated into a carefully woven educational program to provide students the guidance they need to learn in this modern digital world. Thus, we initially wanted to describe some of the issues involved in providing web access and computers or mobile devices, as tools for student learning.

Many teachers today are familiar with laptop usage or usage of other mobile devices that offer Internet connectivity. For example, many teachers and many students own smartphones, so it comes as no surprise that these devices are showing up in schools. What may surprise educators is the use of mobile devices by very young children. Research has suggested that more than half of all children ages five through eight have used a mobile device including smartphones, iPod touch, or iPad ("How to Teach," 2011). Even more interesting is the fact that 19 percent of children ages two through five can operate a smartphone, though only 9 percent can tie their shoes (Frey, Fisher, & Gonzalez, 2011)! This fact alone seems to suggest the advisability of using these devices in the educational setting.

> Web access, coupled with laptop computers or mobile devices, must be integrated into a carefully woven educational program to provide students the guidance they need to learn in this modern digital world.

In order to make these mobile devices user-friendly for teachers, many educational applications have been devised (Gopin, 2012). An *app* is essentially a "short-cut" type of computer program that allows someone to perform a specific, limited type of function. For example, one smartphone app for history teachers presents an interesting fact on "this day in history" that the teacher may use as students enter the history class. Such quick apps make mobile devices much more usable and drastically increase what can be accomplished with a simple smartphone.

In order to be the most effective teachers possible, it is imperative that teachers embrace these technologies, tools which our students are already using. Here's another interesting fact: 65 percent of teens that own their own cell phones attend schools where cell phones are banned, yet they bring these devices to school every day (Frey et al., 2011). As indicated in the introduction, some C2S2 students are demanding the right to use these devices, even in the face of school policies that prohibit such use! Instead of banning these devices, schools should view them as a computing device that they do not have to purchase (Frey et al., 2011). When students are able to use their own mobile device, schools can cut costs on computer labs and lab maintenance (Swistak, 2011).

Data on Efficacy

Prior to the advent of mobile devices, schools were experimenting with "one-to-one laptop" initiatives in which all students were provided with a laptop, and there have been positive results of such one-to-one initiatives (Schwarz, 2012).

Evidence on those initiatives over the last decade has been mixed, with some research showing academic increases and others showing none. However, a consensus has recently been reached that Internet access via either laptops or mobile devices can enhance learning, as long as the hardware tools are well integrated into ongoing best instructional practices. In short, the laptops (or mobile devices) are not enough; they must be well used!

> Nineteen percent of children ages two through five can operate a smartphone, though only 9 percent can tie their shoes.

Still, where these tech tools are well used in ongoing, rigorous instructional procedures, results can be impressive. Schwarz (2012) recently reported on one such initiative whereby students in Grades 3 through 12 were provided with a laptop, and extensive training was provided for teachers to help implement this initiative. Rather than lead the class themselves, teachers were trained to give up some degree of control by letting students work in smaller groups on project-based units. Rather than serve as lecturers (or information delivery agents), teachers became facilitators of learning, with the students focused on laptop screens for much of the school day, exploring problems and working collaboratively to attain solutions. Over a three-year period, many positive results were noted, including increased graduation rates, increased achievement scores in reading, mathematics, and science, and increased attendance. The number of dropouts is down since that initiative began.

While laptop initiatives have been around for at least a decade, the use of mobile devices in the classroom is a more recent trend, and research on efficacy is limited. However, there is positive anecdotal data that supports integrating mobile devices into each classroom. As one example, Project K-Nect, funded through Qualcomm's Wireless Reach Initiative, is a pilot program that was created to examine the use of smartphones in schools (Davis, 2010). Teachers and students in economically challenged Onslow

> Rather than serve as lecturers, teachers should become facilitators of learning, with the students focused on laptop screens for much of the school day, exploring problems and working collaboratively to attain solutions.

County, North Carolina, high schools used smartphones in their math courses in an effort to close the achievement gap. Smartphones were provided to students taking algebra, algebra II, and geometry classes.

The early data shows that C2S2 students receiving smartphones increased their math scores by an average of 20 percent on standardized testing. Other data also supported the smartphones effectiveness; two-thirds of the students are now taking additional math courses and 50 percent of the students reported that they are now considering a career in the math field. Students are also moving on to take more challenging math courses; 90 percent of the original students in the pilot program are enrolled in AP Statistics, a course that is taken by only 1 percent of high school students across the country (Davis, 2010; Tdomf 5d1d9, 2010). These early results display the power that mobile devices have in the classroom to engage and challenge students.

> There is positive anecdotal data that supports integrating mobile devices into each classroom.

Pros and Cons of Wired Teaching

It does not need to be stated that there are pros and cons when allowing students to use laptops or mobile Internet capable devices in the classroom, though most educators today believe that the educational benefits outweigh the potential problems (Davis, 2010; Schwarz, 2012; Xiong, 2011). When deciding to use mobile devices in the classroom, teachers must consider every angle and be prepared to handle them. School leaders and parents may feel that mobile devices distract students from content material, so schools may need to include courtesy as an emphasis within their acceptable use policy, including provisions to prohibit phone usage during teacher or student presentations (Frey et al., 2011). In order to effectively implement the use of mobile devices in classrooms, school districts must take time to teach explicit expectations and students must understand that using the technology is a privilege that can be taken away when abused.

> Early data shows that students receiving smartphones increased their math scores by an average of 20 percent on standardized testing.

One concern with all Internet-capable devices is the ease with which students can find information. In fact, some critics of cell phone use in schools are concerned that students might use the technology to plagiarize more on term papers or cheat during exams. While such concerns are valid and should not be overlooked, there is some evidence that these cautions might be overstated. For example, school leaders at Byron High School, Minnesota, who took part in a pilot program allowing smartphones, had similar concerns initially, but found that in five months of taking part in the program, there was not one incident of cheating or misuse (Swistak, 2011).

Teachers should consider their own classroom expectations when allowing mobile devices in the room. If school districts purchase particular mobile devices, they can opt to have calls and texting features turned off. Filtering particular websites can also limit distractions during class. Individual classroom guidelines should be clear and strictly enforced. Example guidelines include leaving phones out and on top of desks; turning off all phones during tests and exams; and turning down any alerts that students might receive during class time. Again, the acceptable use policy can be expanded to cover these examples of misuse of the technology.

For schools that undertake bring your own device initiatives, the personal devices that students bring to class should be supplemented by a number of laptops or mobile devices provided by the school. In that manner, more students can have Internet access at the same time. Further, the increased use of collaborative group work can alleviate some of the concerns with limited Internet devices. Although many students will probably be able to bring in personal devices for use in the class, not every student will have access. Allowing students to work in groups where at least one student has a device ensures that every student has access to important apps, features, and Internet (Ozuna, 2011).

How Do I Get Started Using Web Access, Laptops, and Mobile Devices?

Step 1: Do Community Relations First!

When schools begin to teach using the Internet, including laptops or mobile devices for Internet access, community relations can become a hot topic locally! Parents, like all American and Canadian citizens, have heard horror stories concerning inappropriate use of the Internet or social networking sites for cyberbullying or sexting, and they are, rightly, very concerned that schools address this issue prior to undertaking a major shift to Internet-based instruction. One school, which obtained a major grant for a one-to-one laptop initiative in Wills Point, Texas, did many hours of community relations prior to purchasing those laptops, in which they carefully explained to parents what firewalls would be in place to protect the students, and how the Internet-capable devices would be used in class. In some districts, prior to using these devices, teachers have had to challenge cell phone bans in particular schools, or find ways to work within the confines of such policies.

The authors at Innovative Educator Blogs advocate first building relationships with key stakeholders including parents, students, other colleagues, and administrators. Educators should ease into mobile device usage with parents and the community by utilizing simple functions on the cell phone to build a bridge between home and school (http://theinnovativeedu cator.blogspot.com/2010/11/ten-building-blocks-to-break-ban-and.html). This might include sending home a text each day so parents are aware of homework assignments or upcoming trips. Teachers can use Twitter to let parents know about the Student of the Week or money due for a field trip. Also, taking time to inform parents displays the educational value of the mobile device in education in a nonthreatening manner.

Step 2: Advocate for Usage Based on Common Core State Standards

Another important component of gathering support is showing how mobile device usage aligns with Common Core State Standards and technology standards in education. The Common Core State Standards (http://www.corestandards.org/the-standards) include many educational standards dealing with technology usage and mobile communications tools for the 21st century classrooms. Further, the International Society for Technology in Education has provided a set of technology standards for educators (http://www.iste.org/standards/nets-for-students.aspx).

Sharing these educational standards and educational goals with parents and the community can be critical in building support for both one-to-one initiative and use of mobile devices in the classroom. Also, make tying the technology emphasis to the move to Common Core State Standards is likely to make any potential community resistance to increased technology easier to work through.

Step 3: Emphasize the Acceptable Use Policy

As described previously, the acceptable Internet usage policy can incorporate many of these concerns and make specific provisions to prohibit many of them. In order to solicit community support, repeated reference to and emphasis of that policy is recommended. As noted previously, we recommend that the policy should require a parent's signature. Such a policy, widely publicized and consistently emphasized, will do a great deal to protect students, as well as to elicit community support for increasing technology in the schools.

Step 4: Start With Simple Communications to Parents

With other stakeholders, including school administration and district teams, it is important for the teacher to become an advocate for change. In order to see change, a teacher must be willing to put in extra time helping with mobile device use contracts, decision making, and recommendations (http://theinnovative educator.blogspot.com/2010/11/ten-building-blocks-to-break-ban-and.html). Teachers may begin by merely using technology to communicate with parents; a simple question such as, "Can I get your e-mail address in case I need to contact you in a hurry?" can go a long way to letting parents know about school use of technology. Using Twitter or other social media for communications can also help parents see that the school is moving forward on the technology front.

Step 5: Begin With Simple Student Assignments

In order to help all stakeholders become comfortable with the mobile device in the classroom, teachers may want to start with small student assignments and invite the parents to observe their child doing the assignments. While many C2S2 students are highly tech-savvy, not all students are, and teachers would do well to remember that. Have students use a personal device as an extra part of a homework assignment. For example, teachers might use a site such as Poll Everywhere, a free web-based service, to ask students a question via mobile phones, Twitter, or the web; or have students respond to tweets about class lectures, under their parent's supervision. Questions about homework, upcoming activities, or class content extend the learning day and provide extra time for students to interact with material. Creating explicit lesson plans to show the advantages of the mobile device will help skeptics concretely see the technology in action.

A part of that process may involve development of a pilot lesson during which the various stakeholders can observe the students using the technology appropriately.

Step 6: Emphasize Web 2.0 Tools and Collaborative Learning

While tech tools can provide an excellent basis for gathering information and research, the Web 2.0 applications that stress collaborative learning should be emphasized. Students have shown through their participation in social network sites such as Facebook, Myspace, and Twitter (all of which are described later in this text) that they crave social interaction, and many Web 2.0 tools are specifically designed to facilitate that collaborative learning. By using only the first four tools described in this book, teachers will gain experience in both tools for Internet-based research and for collaborative teaching. In most cases, it is the collaborative nature of tech-based teaching that truly excites students and transforms the classroom, so we recommend that you reach that point quickly in your tech-teaching journey.

Step 7: Teach Students Repeatedly About Acceptable Usage

In many ways, the easiest stakeholder group to get on board is most likely the students. Still, teachers must take time and work with students to create an acceptable use policy. Teachers can determine the best way to do this based on their class and their students' needs. Teachers might simply create a contract that includes the provisions within the acceptable use policy and have students sign it along with their parents. In order for students to take ownership, however, it may prove beneficial to have students help craft the contract. This would involve giving students the opportunity to thoroughly think through mobile device etiquette and start learning how to use technology responsibly.

Step 8: Seek Outside Funding

The reality over the next decade is that school budgets are likely to be quite limited. However, there are still funds available for supporting technology initiatives, including funding for purchase of laptops or mobility devices. Many grants exist to enable schools and teachers to utilize mobile devices in classrooms, and applying for one or more of these grants might result in significant financial assistance to provide every student with access to a personal handheld device. However, while waiting for grants and other sponsors to help supply technology for the classrooms, teachers and administrators can begin by allowing those students with their own devices to bring them to class, as noted previously. In a class of thirty third-graders, if only six students had their own mobile device, a teacher could create group projects for six groups of five students each, and each group would have collective Internet access.

How Do I Differentiate With These Technology Tools?

It is virtually impossible to catalog all of the ways that laptops, mobile devices, or Internet apps can be used to differentiate instruction in the classroom. In fact, once students obtain Internet connectivity, they tend to differentiate the assignments themselves, as the Internet can offer so very many options for learning. To begin with, we recommend that every teacher in the classroom today become familiar with educational applications that might assist in your specific subject area or grade level, and the compilation of educational apps that can be found on the TCEA website is a great place to begin (Gopin, 2012). See the apps at http://www.tcea.org/ipad.

Here are several examples from the educational literature that show teachers using innovative tech tools for instruction. In many language arts classes today across the country, students meet in small literature circles to discuss novels, poems, and essays. These literature circles provide an opportunity for students to share their thoughts as well as analyze particular content matter found in reading. One language arts teacher in Canada found that allowing students to use mobile devices during these literature circles helped her monitor all of the groups that were meeting simultaneously, a task that had previously been impossible. While each lit circle met, one student used a mobile device to video the conversation. Once the circle time was complete, they used their Bluetooth to send the video to the teacher's phone, allowing her access into each group's conversation (Rapp, 2009). Therefore, the teacher could often see which students needed more assistance in the various groups, and she could provide additional instruction as needed for those specific students.

In science classes, smartphones allow students to access a myriad of information during labs and procedures. Classes studying soil samples in a science lab may only have the resources to concretely observe three to four types of soil. With smartphones, students can use the Internet to search for images of varying soil samples. With more research, students can discover where these soil samples are present and use Google Earth to see satellite images of the soil in various locations around the globe. Students can then use their phones and apps to create charts detailing their findings and upload those to class wikis and blogs. In most cases, students can be allowed to select how they might present their findings, and students with different learning styles and preferences are quite likely to select to present information in the form that best fits their learning style. In that sense, differentiation is taking place, by virtue of the selection of how the student summarizes the data.

However, use of mobile devices is not limited to research in the higher grade levels. Students in primary grades can use mobile devices to increase their understanding of the content matter. In an elementary school math class, students studying shapes can work in small groups to take a scavenger hunt around the school looking for a shape example. Once they locate an example of a shape, they can use their mobile device to take a picture. Using the Internet, the group can then upload the photo to the class wiki (see Tech Tool 4) on shapes and write a brief description proving their example does fit the criteria. Other groups are able to view the wiki and edit or comment on any other group's findings.

Activities such as these take the flat shapes students would typically see in textbooks and turn them into everyday objects—something tangible for the students to understand—and this will increase student engagement with the content under study. Teachers in California's San Diego Unified School District, for example, are currently working under the i21 Interactive Classroom Initiative, a plan to give all students a technology-rich education. According to these teachers, students are more engaged in their work and more enthusiastic in class (Devaney, 2011).

Setting up networks and allowing students to access them with their mobile devices extends the learning day for students and often encourages even the shyest students to share more openly. With mobile devices, students can follow a teacher's tweets and respond to multiple questions about class content. It also provides 24/7 support for students trying to complete homework or study for an exam, since each student can respond and help with any inquiries that are tweeted or posted on class blogs (see Tech Tool 3). Project K-Nect in the Onslow County school district uses a closed social networking site that allows each student to create and post videos. These videos are instructional tools each student creates to explain mathematical concepts and problems. Teachers and students can post pictures as well in order to further explain concepts to students who may need extra help (http://www.projectknect.org/Project%20K-Nect/FAQ .html). These capabilities give students access to help in real time, instead of waiting until the next school day to get help from the teacher.

One final example illustrates how modern technology can enhance a commonly used teaching idea. For the last few decades, teachers have used the idea of providing students with individual "write-on" dry erase boards in class. This is an excellent strategy to get students involved in a particular lesson and allows students to communicate individually with the teacher from across the classroom! A teacher can present a math problem or a multiple choice question and have students write their own responses on the board and simply hold it up for the teacher to see. This enables the teacher to instantly assess student understanding for many students at once, and often provides for relatively private communications indicating a need for individual help. Today, this can be undertaken with technology! With a device such as an iPad or a laptop, teachers can have students use a free painting app (such as Doodle Buddy) to draw their answer, and send that to the teacher. Twitter has been used in classrooms for the same reason—it allows either public or private communication on how well students understand the content.

Examples and Other Useful Resources

A Sample Lesson Plan Using Mobile Devices

We wanted to provide one example of how mobile devices can be built into a lesson plan in a core content area. While some of the shorter examples presented above can also serve as a brief lesson plan, the example below might show how such a lesson plan can be developed, with a specific emphasis on technology usage.

Students will . . .

- Be able to identify the plot found in fiction literature
- Make references to the text to determine the plot
- Summarize major points from text
- Write summary of one section of plot (beginning, middle, or end)
- Create script to enact section of plot with small group
- Use mobile device to record and upload plot section for class review

Materials

- Class book
- Mobile device with video capabilities (smartphone, cell phone, iPad, iTouch)
- Internet access

Set up and prepare

- Ensure that all mobile devices are charged
- Ensure that a class blog or wiki has been created for students to upload final product

Directions

- After class has finished a particular novel or text, discuss with students elements of text including characters, theme, main idea, supporting details, and plot. Discuss with students the elements of a plot including the beginning, middle, and end of the story.
- Divide class into six groups—two for the beginning, two for middle, and two for end.
- Each group will need to summarize its portion of the plot and then write a short script that will enable each group member to be a part of acting out that particular section.
- Have each group use the mobile device to record their final play.
- Once recorded, use wireless capabilities of mobile device to upload the individual sections to the class blog or wiki.
- Have students compare and contrast the two beginnings created, two middles, and two ends. Evaluate the summaries of each group.
- Have students refer back to class blog or wiki to prepare for any tests on text.

Extensions

- Students can also use their script and the audio recording feature of their mobile device to create podcasts. Podcasts can also be uploaded to any class blog or wiki.
- Have one group create an alternate ending to the story and let class members vote on their favorite ending—the alternate one created by classmates or actual ending written by author.

Conclusions

It is not known where technology may take us in the next decades, and as we discussed previously, we considered leaving out this type of discussion altogether from this book, simply because the basic technology tools for access change so quickly. For example, as this book is written, many tech-tool leaders in education are discussing the relative merits of leaving the laptop behind in favor of tablets such as the iPad. However, we ultimately decided that some discussion of laptop initiatives, tablets, mobility devices, and educational apps was appropriate, if for no other reason than to acknowledge that we are all on this journey together, and we all need to strive to remain as current as we can with these tech tools for teaching. With that in mind, we again recommend that teachers begin today and enjoy the journey!

While this section on access and tech tools that facilitate learning provides the basis for learning, we do wish to stress, once again, that the box is not enough! Teachers must integrate tech tools into the curriculum in meaningful ways that guide students in using these powerful tools. The next three tech tools provide an excellent place to begin.

References

Bender, W. N., & Waller, L. (2011). *The teaching revolution: RTI, technology, and differentiation transform teaching for the 21st century.* Thousand Oaks, CA: Corwin.

Davis, M. R. (2010, March 17). Solving algebra on smartphones. *Education Week, 29*(26) 20–23.

Devaney, L. (2011, September 30). Reinventing education; revisited. *eSchool News.* Retrieved from http://www.eschoolnews.com/2011/09/30/reinventing-education-revisited/?

Frey, N., Fisher, D., & Gonzales, A. (2011, October 31). *Literacy 2.0: Reading and writing in 21st century classrooms.* A topical book discussion presented at the annual AuthorSpeak Conference. Solution Tree Press, Indianapolis, IN.

Gopin, L. (2012). *1,000 education apps organized by subject and price.* Retrieved from http://edudemic.com/2012/02/1000-apps

How to teach young children in the digital age. (2011, November 9). *eClassroom News.* Retrieved from http://www.eclassroomnews.com/2011/11/09/how-to-teach-young-children-in-the-digital-age/?

Ozuna, A. (2011, February 18). Please turn on your cell phones before class—part one. *Center for Excellence in Teaching and Learning.* Retrieved from http://www.txwescetl.com/2011/02/please-turn-on-your-cell-phones-before-class-%E2%80%93-part-one

Rapp, D. (2009). Lift the cell phone ban: Stop thinking classroom disruption and start thinking powerful (and free) teaching tool. *Scholastic Administrator.* Retrieved from http://www.scholastic.com/browse/article.jsp?id=3751073

Schwarz, A. (2012). Mooresville's shining example (It's not just about the laptops). *New York Times.* Retrieved from: http://nytimes.com/2012/02/13/education/mooresville-school-district-a-laptop-success-story.html?_r=1

Swistak, S. (2011, May 19). Bryon High School allows Smart phones in classroom. *Kaaltv.com.* Retrieved from http://kaaltv.com/article/stories/s2119877.shtml

Tdomf 5d1d9. (2010, July 9). NC schools use smartphones to close the math achievement gap. *eClassroom News.* Retrieved from http://www.eschoolnews.com/2010/07/09/nc-schools-use-smartphones-to-close-the-math-achievement-gap/

Xiong, B. (2011, September 6). Smartphones, tablets making way into Twin Cities classrooms. *Kare11 News Channel.* Retrieved from http://www.kare11.com/news/article/937325/396/Smartphones-tablets-making-way-into-Twin-Cities-classrooms

Tech Tool 2

Webquests

What Do I Need to Know?

As teachers move into using tech tools for teaching, it is easy to get overloaded for one simple reason; there are so many tech tools out there! One teacher in your building might be using Ning, and another is focused on a Facebook page dedicated to their curricular area. Another may be exploring Google Apps for all writing or project assignments. Teachers then ask themselves, "How should I begin?"

Of course, the amazing number of tech tools available is one reason for the energy in education today. In fact, it is truly an exciting time to be a teacher, and catching the wave of this tech tool revolution in teaching should be one goal for every educator! In short, this is what teaching means in the modern world! Once students have Internet capability in the classroom, we generally recommend three specific tech tools, each of which has been around for a while unlike the tools mentioned above. Our recommended tools are discussed in the next three sections. These recommended tech tools can fit well into virtually every classroom and do not involve a major learning curve for the teacher. In fact, these tools represent the use of tech tools to facilitate ongoing, tried-and-true instructional practices, such as developing themes or projects and researching topics in content areas. Thus, teachers are typically more comfortable using these tools initially. These include the webquest research tool, blogs in the classroom, and the use of wikis to structure today's learning. Of these, both the blog and the wiki represent Web 2.0 tools, in that they allow for and facilitate collaborative work. We can assure you that using only three tech tools is likely to make you a tech leader in your school! Also, your students will become more motivated to complete class assignments and will view your classroom as a modern example of teaching at its best!

Initially, teachers should begin their tech-tool journey by structuring a *webquest* as one requirement within a specific unit of instruction. The concept of a webquest was developed by Bernie Dodge in 1995 (see http://webquest.org/) and many teachers currently use this form of Internet-based research. In most instances, webquests represent the use of Internet sites for gathering information on the topic under study. Thus, most experts would not consider webquests as a true Web 2.0 tool, though some educators would certainly disagree with that general statement.

A webquest is a teacher-structured research experience for the students that is primarily based on use of the World Wide Web and typically takes one or more instructional periods. These research experiences have been used in public school classes since 1995 and focus the student on being able to learn effectively from the uncensored and generally unstructured online universe. Because webquests represent how students will do virtually all of their research through their lifetime, this instructional practice is highly recommended today, and over the years, webquests have provided many exciting opportunities for students to research content online (Bender & Waller, 2011; Ferriter & Garry, 2010).

> **Definition:** A webquest is a teacher-structured research experience for the students that is primarily based on use of the World Wide Web and typically takes one or more instructional periods.

Merely assigning a topic for research and sending students to the computer lab should not be considered a webquest. Rather, webquests are structured by the teacher to introduce information in a reasonable order, gradually increasing the level of information and the demands on the students. Webquests can be either highly structured, or somewhat less focused, depending on the needs of particular students. During the webquest activity, students use prompts, guiding questions, and research links, most of which are typically provided by the teacher, to analyze and synthesize information from the Internet related to their topic of study. Webquests tend to be more effective as educational tools when some structure is provided, but some freedom to explore and create is also provided. In general, teachers should provide guiding questions for some websites but also encourage student exploration. A sample webquest that presents a variety of instructional options is presented at the end of this section. This webquest would probably take four to six instructional periods to complete, but in a two-week instructional unit on Westward Expansion in an American history class, this activity could serve as the initial instructional activities for the first four to six days of that unit.

Rather than structuring the webquest on a narrowly focused topic, teachers can make this a richer tech-based experience by creating

> Webquests tend to be more effective as educational tools when some structure is provided, but some freedom to explore and create is also provided.

questions that use the factual information gleaned from a webquest to focus on the larger concepts and the big ideas within an instructional unit. Note that at the end of the sample webquest, several big themes from the unit were addressed using information gleaned from earlier webquest activities.

Also, websites that allow or encourage students to actually do something are preferable for webquest activities, in contrast to websites from which students merely glean information.

For example, some websites allow students to express their opinions on a topic, take a survey on the topic, or even send an e-mail to someone associated with the topic under study. While not all webquests can include such websites (these websites are quite limited), teachers should include those options when possible. Finally, webquests provide excellent opportunities to teach students several critical skills including (1) how to evaluate their own work as they progress through the webquest, and (2) how to evaluate information they glean from the Internet.

Rubrics are frequently used with webquests to provide students the opportunity to evaluate their own work during the webquest process. Of course, rubrics can be structured in many ways, and not all webquests require rubrics. However, rubrics are recommended, as they help prepare the student for self-evaluation and prevent surprises when the webquest work is evaluated by the teacher. A sample rubric is presented at the end of this section.

Finally, most teachers realize that Internet information, in general, should not be trusted. Of course, some websites are more credible than others, and information that is highly sensationalized, self-serving, or published for profit may be more questionable than other information. In short, the Internet provides a totally uncensored source of data and information, and unless a student is taught how to evaluate that information, this amazing tool will be much less useful. Webquests provide a wonderful opportunity to teach those evaluation skills that provide excellent preparation for the 21st century world. Of course, the level of evaluation skills will change as students progress up through the grade levels, but even very young students can and should be taught, at a minimum, to consider the sources of information they wish to use in school reports and webquests. Noting the name of a website is always advisable, and inquiring into the purpose of an author is a skill that should be taught from the earliest grades. Below, we present a template for a set of general questions that can serve as the beginning of the evaluation process for students in the elementary grades as they evaluate information during a webquest. This may be adapted or edited as needed and then used as a general template for evaluation of research information from both online and more traditional sources.

In the example webquest at the end of this section, we have presented a fairly complicated, five-section webquest, in order to show the potential for a webquest to include many of the topics from an eight-to-ten day instructional unit on US westward expansion. In such an instructional unit, this webquest alone could be used for four to eight days, and could serve as the basis for the entire unit. We also demonstrate here multiple opportunities for differentiating instruction as discussed below.

However, we do recommend that teachers begin with simpler webquests. In fact, most webquests are much simpler than this example. Specifically, if the webquest example included only Section 1, it would be a much simpler webquest, focused on factual and conceptual information from the unit. That webquest would then require only two products from the students. That is the type of rather simple webquest we suggest teachers develop as their first effort.

How Do I Get Started Using Webquests?

We generally recommend that teachers create their first webquest on their own, since such creation is a very effective learning process. Creating a webquest using the specific step-by-step guidelines below will take from forty-five minutes to an hour. However, there are numerous websites available online that can help teachers create their own webquest for any topic. The first two websites below are free for teachers to use, whereas the bottom two websites charge a small fee:

- http://www.kn.pacbell.com/wired/fil
- http://www.zunal.com/
- http://www.teachersfirst.com/exclusives/webquest/
- http://www.internet4classrooms.com/using_quest.htm

Step 1: Select a Topic

Select a topic from an upcoming instructional unit. Webquests can take one day or many days to complete, and in selecting a topic, teachers should consider the timeframe for their planned instruction. Webquests that are merely explorations for factual information on a topic are much quicker educational activities than webquests that require students to create projects. In selecting the topic, teachers should ensure that the topic is broad enough to cover the big ideas within a given instructional unit.

Step 2: Write an Introduction

Teachers should write a brief introduction, typically a paragraph or so, explaining the webquest, and relating the webquest activities to the big ideas in the instructional unit. Instructions for the students should also be included in the introduction. If the introduction is well designed, then webquests can be used as the initial instruction on that content on the very first day of a new instructional unit. Teachers often find that students glean more from this type of initial instructional activity than from a traditional lecture or discussion of a topic, because in the webquest, students are likely to be much more engaged with the lesson content.

Step 3: Identify Appropriate Websites

With the introduction as the focus, teachers can begin to identify one to five websites for students to use in the webquest. These are easy to find by using a search engine, such as Bing, Yahoo, or Google and searching on the topic or topics in the instructional unit. Websites with extensive, high-quality information presented in an efficient way are preferable. While many websites today present information in a video format, use of long video segments is not encouraged, though three- to eight-minute segments can certainly be used.

As noted previously, selecting websites where students actually participate in some activity is preferable to merely using websites as information sources. In civics or government classes, for example, websites from various politicians might be used, since some of these present surveys that allow those politicians to solicit information from their constituents. Other websites offer the option of having students comment on the topic, or even join blogs on the topic of study (see Tech Tool 3—Blogs). Such participation can excite some students about the content. On some websites, students can take a knowledge quiz, and they see their own results immediately online. While such activity-oriented websites cannot be found on every topic in every unit of instruction, including such activities on a webquest is a good idea when they are available.

When beginning the use of webquests, one question that teachers are sure to confront is the use of *Wikipedia* as an information source. *Wikipedia* is a crowd-sourced, online encyclopedia that does include some questionable information since anyone can write content for that source. As the sample webquest below indicates, the teacher that developed this webquest chose to allow students to use *Wikipedia* as a source. While some teachers object to that source since the content is not written by experts, other educators advocate using this source as one way to teach students to evaluate information gleaned from the web (Shapiro, 2010).

Of course, each teacher will make the choice about which websites to specifically identify in the webquest, but almost every teacher will eventually confront the question about using *Wikipedia* as a source of information. We advocate allowing students to use that source, and then teaching those students to carefully evaluate all information used in their project.

Step 4: Develop Guiding Questions

For each of the initial websites used, a set of guiding questions should be developed by the teacher. The initial guiding questions allow the teacher to select and focus the students on the important factual and conceptual content initially. These questions highlight basic information that all students should master and can often be structured by using the Common Core State Standards or state educational standards for the unit under study. Later in the webquest, teachers will develop assignments that encourage more creative activities for the students, but initially, learning the basics of the content is necessary. This distinction between initial questions and later activities begins the scaffolding process within the webquest.

In addition, teachers may wish to place instructions here, along with the guiding questions that let students know how they are expected to complete the assignment. Is the teacher expecting written papers addressing those questions or student contributions to a class wiki or website showing the answers? Questions may be answered on paper and handed in as an independent assignment, or they may be answered in an online format, such as a webquest journal. At any rate, those instructions for assignment completion can be placed here, as shown in the model webquest lesson plan above.

Step 5: Identify Additional Videos and Websites

Student exploration of class topics should always be encouraged, and the identification of appropriate, brief video segments can enrich any webquest. Also additional websites may be identified as optional sources of information for the students. Sources for these videos include YouTube, TeacherTube, The Discovery Channel website, PBS, and other sources on the web. Khan Academy videos (Khan Academy is described in Tech Tool 5) are also useful in this regard in certain subject areas. Encouraging students to explore the topic, by going beyond the narrow focus of the guiding questions, typically creates more excitement for learning, and this will increase student engagement with the content. Also, such exploration by the students often identifies additional sources (e.g., other websites, videos), that teachers can then include in the webquest for future years.

Step 6: Scaffold the Instructional Activities

A wide-open Google search is not a webquest! Rather, a webquest is a teacher-structured learning experience that is designed to take students through their learning, and that requires some degree of scaffolded instruction. In particular, for webquests that present instructional activities over a period of days, those activities should become more complex later in the webquest; and later learning should be built on material previously covered, as the sample webquest lesson plan below demonstrates.

Initially, the guided questions within the webquest should focus on the facts and primary concepts of the instructional unit. After those activities are completed, students should be encouraged to explore the topic in a wider variety of activities that might include creative activities such as development of a newscast or article on the topic, writing a script for a one-act play, or role-playing an interview with certain historical figures, scientists, or characters from literature.

For lower-functioning students, scaffolding the instruction can be critical. Within a webquest, teachers might create somewhat more direct assignments for students with learning challenges. For example, if a video presents the same information as a website text section, more challenged students might be allowed to obtain the answers to the guided questions from the video source. Further, they might also be allowed or encouraged to work with a partner in finding that information, while other students might do that guided question section individually.

> By using webquests, teachers find that they have more time to work with the more challenged students in their class.

Further, teachers might find that, by using webquests, they have more time to work with the more challenged students in their class. When teaching with a webquest, teachers are no longer information providers as they might be in a traditional lecture instructional format. Rather, the webquest makes the teacher's role more similar to that of instructional facilitator, and this typically frees up some teacher time, which can then be devoted to students with learning challenges. At a minimum, the teacher should plan on working through the introduction with these students, in order to ensure that they understand the task and the basic framework of the content under study. Thus, the teacher can provide herself as a scaffolding support for those students.

Step 7: Create an Evaluation Rubric

Rubrics have long been used in education for grading, and most teachers are familiar with this evaluation process. However, we would point out that rubrics are more important in the context of assignments that are not teacher-directed, so rubrics are highly recommended for all webquests. In short, rubrics can let students know what is expected in various assignments or subassignments within a webquest. Further, when students are working in groups, rubrics can often help the group stay on task and focused on getting the required work completed. Even though the webquest may include specific assignments that are not completed by all students, rubrics can still be developed that will help guide the work. A template and sample rubric is presented at the end of this section for the webquest on the Battle of the Little Bighorn.

Step 8: Plan a Minilesson on Evaluation of Internet Sources

In webquests, as in many online assignments, students will be accessing and using some content that is uncensored. This is vastly different from only a few decades ago, when students accessed information primarily from only three sources—textbooks, encyclopedias in media centers, and teachers. In those days, information was "controlled" in the sense that most information was evaluated for accuracy and balance prior to the student accessing it, and while that may have been less true in the case of information provided by teachers, it is still a fact that most information available to students was evaluated for them.

Of course, those days are long gone. Today, it is

> In previous decades, students accessed information primarily from only three sources—textbooks, encyclopedias in media centers, and teachers, so information was evaluated for accuracy and balance prior to the student accessing it.

extremely rare to see students doing a report or theme paper by trotting down to the media center and looking in an encyclopedia! Rather, they go online to look for information, and every educator today knows that this is exactly the skill that they will need throughout their lives when using the Internet. Also, many other tech tools will require that students know how to evaluate information that they access.

In short, it is essential that students be taught how to evaluate information they get from various Internet sources, and webquests provide an excellent vehicle for such instruction. We recommend that teachers teach a "minilesson" on evaluation of information, and provide students with guidelines that focus the student not only on the website where the information was found, but also on the author, his intent in preparing the information, any controversies or disagreements in the information, and any contrary positions or arguments. The Template for Evaluation of Information Obtained from the Internet provided at the end of this section can be printed out, edited, and used for that instruction.

However, it is critical that teachers teach this more than just once. Evaluation of information from an uncensored and often unreliable source, as much of the information on the Internet can be, is a critical 21st century skill, so it certainly should be taught diligently initially, and then stressed throughout the year.

How Do I Differentiate With Webquests?

We suggest that you develop differentiated assignments within your webquests, as indicated in the sample webquest lesson plan below. Webquests typically include different types of activities; some are individual activities, and others are team-based or partner activities, and the later offers an excellent learning opportunity for interpersonal learners. Further, differentiation according to other learning styles and preferences can be addressed in the webquest. In the sample webquest lesson plan below, some activities require highly developed linguistic skills (e.g., writing a newscast or a script for a one-act play), whereas others require spatial intelligence and highly developed visualization skills (drawing a battlefield map). In short, in developing the webquest, teachers should differentiate the assignments by including a variety of different activities that involve various learning styles, and then helping students choose activities that are appropriate for them.

Examples and Other Useful Resources

A Sample Webquest Lesson Plan

Westward Expansion and the Battle of the Little Bighorn

This webquest is designed to help you understand the Battle of the Little Bighorn, the Sioux War of 1876, and westward expansion from 1865 through 1890. We need to know how that battle represented and impacted the concept of Manifest Destiny that governed much of American history during the last thirty years of the 1800s. All students will complete two sections from this webquest and may also choose to complete Section V, the optional extra credit assignment. Initially, all students are required to complete Section I below, and then all students will complete at least one additional section. The teacher will help you select which additional sections to complete, and some weight will be given to students' choices on which sections they complete.

I. Section One: Battle of the Little Bighorn and the Sioux War of 1876
   Resources:

   http://en.wikipedia.org/wiki/Battle_of_the_Little_Bighorn

   http://www.eyewitnesstohistory.com/custer.htm

   http://en.wikipedia.org/wiki/Manifest_Destiny

   A. Using these Websites, make notes about the facts about the battle.

      1. Why was this battle fought?
      2. Who were the leaders? (Three Native Americans and three cavalry officers)
      3. Who was the aggressor in this battle?
      4. How large were the opposing forces?
      5. Describe in three or four sentences the plan for General Custer's attack.
      6. Did the weapons used by each side impact the fight? Explain your answer.
      7. Why did Custer split his forces? How many groups did he create when he split his forces (Note: Do not confuse Custer's splitting of his forces with the other large columns of soldiers moving toward the battle).

8. Who led each of the forces once Custer split his command?
9. Is splitting one's forces in battle usually a good idea? Explain your answer.
10. Relative to the battle itself, who lost and what was lost?
11. Relative to the Sioux War of 1876, who lost and what was lost?

B. Battle Diagram: After writing answers to these questions, diagram the overall attack of Custer's forces, pointing out positions of the leaders in the battle.

II. Section Two: News Article Script! The Aftermath of This Battle and the Sioux War of 1876.

Using the websites above, and others you may find, answer each of the following questions in one or two paragraphs. These should be written as if they were to become a newspaper article on this fight that actually appeared in a newspaper in 1876. You must present your sources, and like a news article, present any differences of opinion in the story.

A. How did Custer's defeat impact the nation?
B. What were the consequences for the Native Americans of this battle and this war?
C. How does this battle and this war relate to the concept of Manifest Destiny?
D. How did this fight impact westward expansion of the American nation?

III. Section Three: Defending Their Actions

Each team of students will choose one task below, develop a one-act play in which the following characters present their thoughts, and then each team will videotape that play and include it on the class wiki or school website.

A. Your task is to prepare a one-act play in which both Benteen and Reno defend their actions in the Battle of the Little Bighorn before a military board. They must address questions about their actions.
1. Why did Reno retreat across the river?
2. Why did they not seek to join Custer on his end of the battlefield to help and possibly save him?

B. Prepare a one-act play in which both Crazy Horse and Sitting Bull provide testimony to a congressional inquiry board. They should address the questions such as the following:
1. Why did they fight Custer at the Little Bighorn River?
2. What was their view of Custer?
3. What was their view of Manifest Destiny?
4. Why did they leave the reservation?
5. How did that battle impact their people?

IV. Section Four: Different Views of Custer

Resource: Also view a seven-minute video at video.pbs.org/video/2185377825.

A. Obtain a copy of a movie called *Little Big Man* and watch it. Then write a five-paragraph theme that addresses the questions below.

1. Was Custer a reasonable man, as portrayed here?
2. When was this movie made, and what events were ongoing in world history at that time that might have impacted this Hollywood view of Custer?
3. Would this Hollywood portrayal been popular in the 1940s or 1950s? Explain your answer.
4. Did Custer's actions help or hinder the greater goal of the US government in realizing Manifest Destiny?

B. Obtain a copy of *Custer's Last Stand* from the PBS website above or the local library. Using that as a source, develop a five-paragraph theme and address the same questions as above.

V. Section Five: Open Web search

As an extra credit option, students working individually or in teams of two or three may obtain a minimum of two additional websites on this battle or the Sioux War of 1876 and complete the following task:

In addition to Manifest Destiny, various other factors impacted westward expansion, including construction of transcontinental railroads, the search for gold and silver, the desire of settlers for farmland, and the Mexican War of 1848. Search for information on one of these factors, and develop a five-minute PowerPoint report on it for the class wiki.

A Sample Rubric for Evaluation of the Webquest

Evaluation of Section I:

4. All questions were answered accurately and in great detail, and the battlefield map diagram was accurate and neat.
3. All questions were answered accurately in some detail, and the map was accurate.
2. All questions were answered but more detail would be desirable. The map was acceptable but not clear.
1. Most of the questions were answered but more detail is needed, and the map was not clear. This work will need to be redone.
0. The answers lacked detail and some were inaccurate. The map was not acceptable. This work will need to be redone.

Evaluation of Section II:

4. All factual questions were answered in an engaging detail that would keep a reader's interest throughout the story. Sources were described and different opinions were presented and defended.
3. All factual questions were answered adequately, but the organization was not as tight as a news article typically requires. Sources were described but various opinions need more attention.
2. Most factual questions were answered but more detail is needed, and organization must be tighter. Sources were not described well, but various opinions need more attention.
1. Most of the factual questions were answered, but some were not accurate, and the organization was not effective. No sources were cited and differing opinions were not presented. This work will need to be redone.
0. The answers lacked detail or questions were left unaddressed. This work will need to be redone.

Evaluation of Section III:

4. The play was well-developed and entertaining. All required data was presented accurately in a very neat dialogue, and the data were gleaned from a minimum of two sources that supported each other.
3. The play was well-developed and presented all relevant detail accurately. Two sources were in evidence, but there was some unresolved evidence that should be addressed more effectively.
2. The play was well done, but there were some factual errors in the testimony. Also, more should have been done to support the testimony in each case.
1. The play was not clear on the perceptions or positions of the characters, and more attention must be given to sources and evaluation of the information from them. This work will need to be redone.
0. This play was not at all clear. Sources were not explored and the testimony was not factual. This will need to be redone.

Evaluation of Section IV:

4. The theme was well-developed and well-structured. All questions were answered accurately and in great detail.
3. The theme was well-developed and well-structured, but more attention needs to be given to one or more of the questions.
2. The theme organization was not as effective as needed, but all questions were addressed.
1. The theme was not structured well, and several questions were not addressed or answered accurately. This work will need to be redone.
0. The theme was poorly structured, and many answers lacked detail. This work will need to be redone.

Evaluation Scores: Each student's score may range from 0 to 8. Every student should receive a grade on Section I above and a grade on one additional section. Also students will receive 1 point for completing the extra credit assignment. You should add your scores together below to find your total score on this webquest. Total scores of 5 and above are considered passing: 5 = D, 6 = C, 7 = B, and 8 = A.

My score: Section I _____

Additional Section _____

Extra Credit _____

My Total Score: _____

Guidelines for Evaluation of Information Obtained From the Internet

1. What is the website you are using? Is this from a news website, a political website, or a website that advocates for any specific agenda? Remember to copy down the entire website as your source while you are there.

2. Is the position of this author stated clearly and succinctly? Is there ambiguity in what the author is trying to say?

3. Is this information written by someone who is identified? Is it a blog or an opinion of only one reader?

4. Is the information credited to or cited from another source? If so, is that a reputable source?

5. Is evidence provided to support the author's position? What is the quality of that evidence? How many separate evidence-based points does the author make to argue for his or her position? Make a note of those.

6. Are there counterarguments to the position of this author? Are those stated here and addressed? Have you found counterpoints here or elsewhere that were not addressed? If so, can you have confidence that the source that omitted those arguments is believable?

7. Is the evidence believable? Is the overall position of the author believable? This is sometimes called the "smell test," which means essentially, does this person's perspective, position, or argument "stink" too much to be believable?

8. Are all sides of the issue discussed fairly? Are there sides of the issue, question, or topic that are not addressed in this work?

9. Does this author have a particular perspective that you can identify? Is that perspective self-serving in any way? Is the author open and honest in presenting his or her perspective, and does that perspective lead to fairness or overt bias in the work you are using?

10. Have you identified other sources that present the same ideas? Is there a consensus on the issue or topic you are studying that you can identify?

11. Is expert opinion or expert testimony presented? If so, who is the expert, and does his or her expertise relate directly to the question at hand?

12. Is celebrity endorsement used in this work? What value can you ascribe to that celebrity endorsement? Does the celebrity have celebrity based on an area of expertise directly related to the topic you are studying?

13. Is the content you are reading sensationalized in any way? Is inflammatory language used that seems highly questionable?

Conclusions

The webquest is one of the original tech tools, having been around since the 1990s, and we do urge all teachers to begin using webquests as soon as computer availability allows in their school. As explained herein, teaching students to complete webquests emphasizes much more than the specific content under study, by stressing evaluation of information from the Internet, and save use of the World Wide Web. For these reasons, the webquest is one of the first tech tools that we encourage teachers to try.

References

Bender, W. N., & Waller, L. (2011). *The teaching revolution: RTI, technology, and differentiation transform teaching for the 21st century.* Thousand Oaks, CA: Corwin.

Ferriter, W. M., & Garry, A. (2010). *Teaching the iGeneration: 5 easy ways to introduce essential skills with web 2.0 tools.* Bloomington, IN: Solution Tree Press.

Shapiro, M. (2010). Embracing Wikipedia. *Education Week, 29*(31), 5.

Tech Tool 3

Blogs

What Do I Need to Know?

A *blog* is an online journal where posted information from both teachers and students is arranged and archived in reverse chronological order (Ferriter & Garry, 2010). Using a blog, teachers and students can work individually or together to create and self-publish content on the topic under study and create links to other documents and videos online. Blogs provide the opportunity for connectivity in that the students can leave comments on each post. When teachers create classroom blogs, students are able to interact with classroom content long after the school day has ended.

> **Definition:** A blog is an online journal where posted information from both teachers and students is arranged and archived in reverse chronological order.

The value of the social learning fostered by this tech tool, as well as others described later in this book, is hard to overstate. Today's C2S2 kids absolutely love doing schoolwork in a collaborative fashion (Richtel, 2012), and they are much more motivated to complete homework when it involves collaborative blog postings or other online work. In fact, students are demonstrating by their behavior that they enjoy social interactions online, and teachers must tap into that power for improving education in the classroom. To check that statement for yourself, we'd suggest that you merely ask any group of students (we suggest Grade 5 and higher) how many of them have a Facebook page! Use that simple test, and then consider the nature of the C2S2 learners in your own school. Their answer, as much as anything else, is likely to convince you that using their desire to network can be of benefit in motivating them to explore the topics you teach, and a blog is the simplest way to do that. In fact, the very popularity of the social networking sites available today demonstrate students' desire to be connected and utilizing class blogs fills that desire for socially-mediated learning by offering high levels of student-to-student interaction (Bender & Waller, 2011; Richtel, 2012). As you will see, many of the tech tools described later in this book also provide that same advantage.

Blogging and Professional Development

Blogging has become an excellent way to share information. As one example, the second author of this book does a blog for new, expecting mothers in conjunction with a local Onslow County Hospital in North Carolina (the *Onslow MomTalk's TummyTime* blog). This is a blog for pregnant women and women with infants and consists of a community of bloggers who wish to share or gather information from each other or merely share struggles, triumphs, and good ideas during pregnancy and infancy. Like most blogs, this blog does show the basic outline of a blog where entries are archived by date, posts are succinct, and images and media are included. Most of these blog entries are "content rich" for women who wish to seek information on a variety of related issues.

To view this sample blog go to http://tummytime.onslow.org/tummy time/. On the left hand side of the screen you will see the various authors of these blogs. To find the blog above, hover over the pictures until you see the name Laura Waller displayed and click on that picture. As this example indicates, you can find content rich information on blogs that addresses almost any topic.

As you might imagine, there are literally thousands of blogs for educators, on a wide variety of topics in education. For example, a recent online article provided a list of the fifty most popular blogs for teachers (http://edudemic.com/2011/12/teacher-blogs/), and that might be an excellent place to start. In the area of technology in the classroom, two of these have been followed by thousands of teachers, blogs by Will Richardson (http://willrichardson.com/) and William Ferriter (http://teacherleaders.typepad.com/the_tempered_radical/). Both of these teachers are leaders in educational technology for the classroom, and we can recommend these blogs as sources for effective teaching ideas. Also, the blog by Vicki Davis, the *Cool Cat Teacher,* (http://coolcatteacher.blogspot.com/p/advertise.html) is another great blog for teachers to follow.

Classroom Blogs

In addition to teacher blogs, using a blog for student discussions is one hallmark of a 21st century classroom. To use a blog in this fashion, teachers simply write a post about a particular topic and have students respond to it on the blog. Students may make responses to the teacher or to entries of other students, so the blog tends to be quite collaborative in nature. Blogs are highly accessible as students can log onto blogs via personal computers, mobile devices, or any other technology tool that has Internet capabilities. Students even have the option to "follow" blogs so that the students would be notified via e-mail whenever there is a change on the blog itself. As compared to a standard webpage, blogs are frequently updated with concise posts making information on the blog both highly relevant and up to date.

There are many uses for a blog in the classroom, but these uses tend to fall into three general categories: blogs used for communications, blogs used for instruction, and blogs that do both. For communication purposes, blogs can be used to keep students and parents informed of all that is going on in the classroom. Instead of the standard newsletter or note to parents, both of which may not make it home, the blog will provide timely information for the family. Teachers can post homework assignments, announcements, class requirements, and handouts for specific content. Students and parents can use the blog as a board for questions and answers with the teacher.

From the instructional perspective, blogs provide an excellent opportunity for further class discussion, and collaborative work by the students. This can be a great way to increasingly involve students who might be somewhat hesitant to participate in class. Research has shown that students prefer writing in class blogs in comparison to other types of writing assignments (Richtel, 2012). Also, since students can post their work in their own time frame, there is no pressure for anyone to react quickly, providing time for students to reflect on their answer before posting ("Blog Basics," 2012). Students can also use the class blog to collaborate on class assignments by posting documents for peer review and teacher comment. As students upload more individual work, the blog serves as an ongoing digital portfolio where progress can be analyzed over time in the archives ("Blog Basics," 2012).

> There are many uses for a blog in the classroom, but these tend to fall into three general categories: blogs used for communications, blogs used for instruction, and blogs that do both.

How Do I Get Started Using Blogs?

Step 1: Select a Blog Hosting Site

First, teachers must select a blogging host website for their blog. Fortunately, there are numerous websites that assist in the creation of a blog, and some are available at no cost (see the options at the end of this section). However, you should select a blog host that is best suited to your needs. Some blog hosts are ad-free and some offer higher levels of privacy by requiring passwords and login information from students and teachers. Teachers should choose a blog that meets their needs, and initially we recommend using a secure blog that only class members, the teacher, and the parents can access.

Step 2: Always Consider Student Security

For that reason, we generally recommend using a blog that requires login information, because these ensure higher levels of security for students. Passwords can be given out to the school community and parents so that there is a large audience able to access and read the blog. Making blogs available to the school and parent community encourages students to think about their audience and how to engage them, and it fosters student excitement about using the blog (Bender & Waller, 2011; Richtel, 2012). Instead of writing a research paper that only the teacher will see, students using blogs are able to create work that is shared with a much larger audience, and that ultimately increases their motivation and commitment to the writing project.

Step 3: Consider Distinctions

However, Richtel (2012) has also pointed out that blog entries are, typically, much shorter than are themes or term papers, and the latter types of assignments require students to organize their written arguments in a much more complex and systematic fashion. For this reason, while blogging is encouraged in virtually every classroom, the use of blogs in the classroom should not result in elimination of writing assignments that require longer and more sustained, organized efforts (Richtel, 2012). In the 21st century world, C2S2 students will be required to do both types of writing, so both should be emphasized in our teaching.

Step 4: Follow Blog Host Instructions

Each blog host offers step-by-step instructions on how to set up a classroom blog. We recommend that teachers look at one or two of these blog hosts and watch the tutorial videos on that website in order to learn the tips and tricks of that particular blogging host. Most blog sites will have teachers enter basic account information including name, address, and e-mail address. Teachers can then review the privacy options and use those to determine who can access the blog (e.g., only members of your class or class members and their parents?). Once a level of privacy is decided on, blogging hosts offer a template so that anyone can point, click, and post to the blog. When creating a post, the blogger will choose a post title and simply enter the content. Links to outside documents, websites, videos, pictures, and audio clips can also be included in the blog.

> Blog entries are, typically, much shorter than are themes or term papers, and the latter types of assignments require students to organize their written arguments in a much more complex and systematic fashion.

How Do I Differentiate With Blogs?

Blogs make differentiating instruction easier by providing ways to differentiate the content, the learning process, or the learning product. Let's imagine a fourth-grade North Carolina science classroom where students must work to "build an understanding of the composition and uses of rocks and minerals." The teacher may have several students in her class who require extra intervention in science as well as a few students who need extra challenge. In order to differentiate the content, the teacher may teach about the characteristics and properties of three basic minerals in class. After the initial class conversation, the teacher would have the students needing enrichment log onto the class blog where she posted a link to videos about several more minerals. Students would be able to post questions and comments on the blog about these minerals. At the same time, those students needing extra intervention would find a link on the blog to a video about the same three minerals discussed in class. These students would be able to review the same content and post any further questions or comments on the blog. In this manner, the teacher is able to differentiate the content through the use of the interactive class blog without embarrassing any students in a class setting.

Blogs can also help differentiate the process used in the classroom. Since teachers and students can link any digital documents, audio, and video clips to a class blog, many learning options are offered for students with different learning styles that may not be offered in the traditional classroom setting. Material presented in class can be differentiated on the blog for students who may need a more visual representation of the content or need extra time with the material in an auditory manner. Teachers may

> Blogs make differentiating instruction easier by providing ways to differentiate the content, the learning process, or the learning product.

choose to use the class blog as an extra resource for students by posting audio clips, videos, graphics, and extra links to documents for some students. Students can then search out the medium that helps them understand the content in a clear manner, allowing them to use a process that facilitates their learning in the most effective manner possible.

Blogs also provide an opportunity to differentiate the required product that demonstrates understanding. Since documents can be linked to the blog, there may be various links for different student groups. Looking back at the North Carolina science classroom, one group may find a link to a webquest that would further challenge their study of minerals and their webquest answers would demonstrate their understanding of the content (for more information on webquests check Tech Tool 2—Webquests). Another group may access a link on the blog to a word document that has a standard question and answer quiz on the mineral compositions they studied in class and online. Once the quiz is completed, the students can print off their answers and turn in their work. Finally, another group may have a link to a video on minerals with several questions that the students have to respond to on the blog. All of these measures could be utilized to assess student understanding of the original content. Again, the teacher in that science classroom is able to choose which required product would be best suited for each individual student.

Examples and Other Useful Resources

A Sample Lesson Plan Using Blogs

Typically, we do not recommend the creation of a blog as a lesson activity; rather we recommend that teachers use blogs to present information and to follow up assignments and class discussions. Blogs are also useful for evaluation (i.e., grading student's posting to the class blog throughout a given instructional unit), and for home-school connections. Here are just a few ways you could use a blog in your classroom.

- After reading a chapter on the water cycle in class, students log on to the blog to watch a video on TeacherTube depicting the water cycle. Students may then be required to post comments or reflections to the blog and comment on the postings of other students.
- Send home access information so that parents can log onto the blog for homework assignments, field trip announcements, and class calendars.
- Use the blog as a "book review" tool by having students write and post reviews of books that they are reading. Students may then use their peers' book reviews to choose their next book.
- Prior to beginning a science experiment, have students post their hypothesis on the experiment. Students will then be able to return to the blog and evaluate their hypothesis when the experiment is complete.
- When studying various shapes in mathematics, have students use their mobile devices to upload examples of the shapes they see in the community or in their home onto the blog, with a comment on what shape it is and why it is interesting.
- In a civics or government class, post a link to political debates and have students critique political statements and agendas.
- In a history class, teachers might have students interview one person from a different generation about the similarities and differences in high schools now and then. Students can then post the responses on the blog.

Blog Hosting Sites for Teachers

http://www.classblogmeister.com

This is a free website designed specifically for teachers and classroom use. All articles and comments are sent to the teacher for approval prior to being published, which helps the teacher ensure acceptable behavior on the blog. Teachers can also ensure that the site is password protected.

https://www.21classes.com/

21 Classes is a blog host with several options for teachers. A single teacher blog is free for teachers and provides the teacher with a central dashboard for controlling accounts and comments. This free option allows for uploads of videos and images. The blog can be made public or private for the classroom. Regardless of the setting, the teacher has control over which posts are approved and even if certain posts are only approved for certain groups. 21 Classes also offers fee-based programs where students have their own personal blogs monitored by the teacher.

http://edublogs.org/

Edublogs is another host created entirely for educational use. It allows teachers to make their blogs private or public. Edublogs boasts an adult-content free site, making it safe for students to browse through the site. There are several options for teachers when using Edublogs. The free version allows students to create their own blog without having an e-mail address. The site recommends that a single teacher use the Pro version, which is $3.33 a month for fifty student blogs as well. This Pro version has more options for teacher monitoring.

http://education.weebly.com/

Weebly is a free service for teachers. Due to the emphasis on education, no advertising appears on the blogs. The service is completely free for up to forty student accounts. The host supports picture, video, document, and photo gallery uploads. All websites (either teacher- or student-created) have the option to be password protected, offering higher levels of security for parents and teachers. Weebly boasts an easy drag-and-drop editor, making the creation of any site easy.

Conclusions

While blogs have been around for a while, many teachers have yet to use them, as many schools do not have either wifi or computer availability. However, blogging has become rather mainstream, and teachers can find blogs on almost any topic whatsoever. Further, while some C2S2 students might see blogging as rather "old school," this is a tech tool that is relatively easy to initiate, and we encourage all teachers to explore blogging in conjunction with their classes.

References

Bender, W., & Waller, L. (2011). *The teaching revolution: RTI, technology, and differentiation transform teaching for the 21st century.* Thousand Oaks, CA: Corwin.

Blog Basics. (2012). *Teaching Today.* Retrieved from http://teachingtoday.glencoe.com/howtoarticles/blog-basics

Ferriter, W. M., & Garry, A. (2010). *Teaching the iGeneration: 5 easy ways to introduce essential skills with web 2.0 tools.* Bloomington, IN: Solution Tree Press.

Richtel, M. (2012, January 20). Blogs vs. term papers. *New York Times.* Retrieved from http://www.nytimes.com/2012/01/22/education/edlife/muscling-in-on-the-term-paper-tradition.html?_r=1

Tech Tool 4

Wikis

What Do I Need to Know?

For decades, teachers have posted student's work on the class bulletin board. Today, many teachers have also had the experience of posting exemplary student work to their school's website, which can enable parents and grandparents to view that successful work. As mentioned in the previous section on blogs, C2S2 students love to see their successful work displayed, and this is highly motivational for many students across the grade levels. However, today, teachers are finding that they can establish what is essentially a private website for their own class. They can also let parents, other teachers, or everyone view the work done in their class. A wiki is an editable website, usually with limited access, that allows students to collaboratively create and post written work or digital files, such as digital photos or even digital video (Watters, 2011).

> **Definition:** A wiki is an editable website, usually with limited access, that allows students to collaboratively create and post written work or digital files, such as digital photos, or even digital video.

Wikis have been used in some classrooms since about 1995 (Watters, 2011; Richardson, 2010), though many teachers have yet to use a wiki because of limited technology availability. However, as schools increase Internet connectivity and more technology reaches the classroom, wikis are certainly a teaching tool that every teacher should consider (Richardson, 2010; Waller, 2011). In one sense, a wiki can be used as a combination of a unit syllabus and instructional activities for students, and some teachers today do all of their instruction based within wikis because wikis are so versatile. Indeed, both of the first two tech tools described in this book, webquests and blogs, can be embedded within a class wiki, along with virtually any other type of class assignment teachers might imagine.

As described in the last section, a class blog lists and preserves all students' and teachers' posted comments separately, usually in chronological order. This can facilitate collaboration, but with comments listed separately, students generally cannot work on the same document. However, by using a wiki, teachers can encourage true student collaboration, since in the wiki, C2S2 students can edit the work of others collaboratively within the same document or digital file. Of course, this makes a wiki a true Web 2.0 tool, since collaborative options can be explored in wikis that have not been possible previously. Thus, when a group is working together on a report or class presentation and a student wishes to contribute a thought or idea in that work, they merely edit and extend the work done previously by others, embedding their idea directly in that work. This functionality makes wikis an excellent tech tool for increasing the types of collaboration and social learning that students today enjoy. Also, most wikis allow teachers to track every posted entry to see who is making entries and who in the class is not, and even in collaborative work, that feature is quite useful for following individual student contributions.

> Both webquests and blogs can be embedded within a class wiki, along with virtually any other type of class assignment teachers might imagine.

The online encyclopedia *Wikipedia*, which was mentioned previously, is probably the most widely recognized of all wikis. In *Wikipedia*, anyone in the world can choose to edit any information on any topic, and if their edit is factually incorrect, or they state something that is simply wrong, other users are quite likely to edit out the error, often in a matter of minutes. The term *crowdsourcing* has become popular in the tech lingo to mean that the crowd or worldwide group of persons contributing to *Wikipedia* can all be considered as authors of the *Wikipedia* content—thus crowd-sourcing.

> *Wikipedia* is probably the most widely recognized of all wikis.

Wikis for Professional Development

Today, there are many wikis online and most are devoted to one specific topic. Those topics range across the wide scope of human interest (e.g., travel in Texas, favorite holiday recipes, nature photography). Wikis allow persons to share ideas, and develop content together, and, like *Wikipedia*, if someone posts something that is not correct, later users are likely to correct that factual error in the content. In fact, unlike written texts, wikis are usually self-correcting.

For an example of an informational wiki for teachers, you might wish to review a wiki created by the second author of this book. This wiki shares information teachers might find useful on professional development in technology and differentiated instruction. Please feel free to visit this wiki and use it as a guide when creating your own. You will notice that there is a home page for general introduction and then tabs on the right-hand side of the wiki that indicate the material available. Teachers can browse the wiki and then add in their own information and resources. To visit this wiki go to http://laurawaller.wikispaces.com/.

Wikis in the Classroom

In addition to this type of professional development exchange of ideas with wikis, they are also very applicable in almost any classroom. In fact, wikis encourage students to publish their own work contributions and edit anyone else's content in a relatively ungoverned fashion. Over time, this leads to an online, collaborative community of information providers, and most inaccuracies within the wikis are eventually corrected by later users. Now imagine the power of this collaboration in your classroom! Using wikis for instruction will motivate your students to increase participation; this tech tool can truly energize and excite students in multiple ways in comparison to traditional assignments or group projects. Again, students are demonstrating by their actions that they love social networking, and using that motivation for increased social exchange, teachers can use a wiki to encourage students to participate more fully in classroom and homework.

In developing written or video content for the wiki, students learn how to work together, sort through information, evaluate information using other sources, create newly synthesized information, and make contributions to the content already on the wiki, all clearly skills that 21st century learners will need throughout life (Waller, 2011). Because students today are inundated with information on a daily basis, it is the responsibility of teachers to teach students how to sift through information, evaluate the validity, determine the purpose of the author, and contribute their own findings and research in the digital world. Wikis provide one format for learning and applying these critical skills (Richardson, 2010).

> Wikis serve one function for teachers, perhaps better than any other teaching tool: wikis are excellent for teaching subject-area vocabulary.

Further, wikis serve one function somewhat better than any other teaching tool: wikis are excellent for teaching subject-area vocabulary. Virtually all teachers from Grade 4 and up spend some time teaching vocabulary in the content areas, but wikis can save that time! Within a wiki, teachers can merely list the vocabulary terms for the unit, and have students define and provide examples. Students can pick up the definitions for each term as they work through the wiki for that unit! In the wiki steps presented herein, note that teachers merely list vocabulary terms on an unlocked wiki page and let students define them. By requiring that such work be completed on the class wiki, the teacher saves valuable class time. Students still get the content, however, in a manner similar to their use of *Wikipedia!* Most students enjoy this type of activity and will learn vocabulary terms based on this activity, without the teacher having to take additional class time to teach content-specific vocabulary.

How Do I Get Started Using Wikis?

Teachers who have never used a wiki previously can set up a wiki for their class in approximately thirty to forty-five minutes. Further, the Internet provides many sites that will assist teachers in developing and using wikis. Here are a few that you can investigate, along with our recommendations for beginning. Of course, each site below involves slightly different procedures for creating your wiki, so we recommend a specific, free wiki site for your initial work. Still, any of these wiki support websites are fine, and if a teacher in your building is using another site, by all means, partner with that teacher and use that website. Here are several that are frequently used by educators:

- http://plans.pbworks.com/signup/edubasic20
- http://wikisineducation.wetpaint.com/
- http://www.teachersfirst.com/content/wiki/wikistep2.cfm

While any of the sites above can help, we prefer the wikispaces website, so this step-by-step guide is based on using that site (www.wikispaces.com). Wikispaces provides free, private wikis for educators, and 7 million teachers and students currently use this site for wikis in education. Let's look over a sample wiki, then each of you will begin to create one. In order to help you learn how to use this wiki, we recommend that you review brief videos from the wikispaces homepage (http://www.wikispaces.com/content/wiki-tour).

On the wikispaces homepage, you can find many demonstration videos to choose from, but the first two that we do recommend are called "Introduction" and "Creating Educational Wikis." These are very brief and will help you in understanding the creation of a wiki.

Step 1: Select a Free Wiki Site

Once you are online, you should begin by going to the wikispaces website (http://www.wikispaces.com/site/for/teachers). Once this site is accessed, teachers will need to select a username, password, and a wikispace name. There is an option for teachers to create a free wiki for their class, toward the lower right of the wikispaces homepage. Click there to begin.

Step 2: Set Up a "Students Only" Wiki to Begin With

We recommend that teachers create either a protected wiki (a wiki which everyone can view, but only class members can edit), or a private wiki (only

Figure 4.1

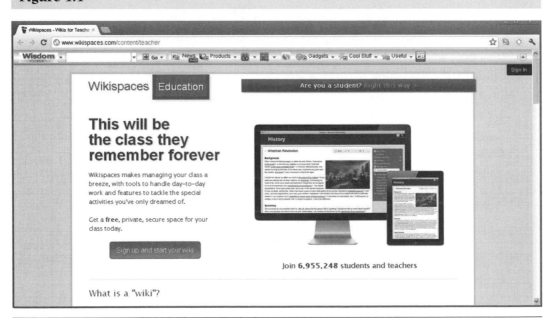

Source: Wikispaces © 2012 Tangient LLC

class members can view and edit). The private wiki option is free for educators. While you may wish to experiment with more public wikis later, you should start with something only your class can enter.

Step 3: Create a Wiki Homepage

We recommend that each wiki include a homepage as the first page within the wiki. This page will include a brief introduction to the unit of study and other basic information. First, teachers should create a title for the wiki and put that on top of the homepage. Simply type in an appropriate unit title and highlight it. Then click on the "Heading" function at the top of the page, select "Level One Heading." That will bold the heading and increase its size.

Next, each title page should have an opening or introductory paragraph. This should be a paragraph-long description of the content and purpose of the wiki. You should phrase this paragraph as an "interest grabbing" paragraph, and using questions is very appropriate. Also, relating the information in the coming unit to the past unit or interesting topics is important.

Step 4: Add Videos or Digital Photos

Again, the goal of the homepage is to excite the interest of the students. We suggest you add a set of interesting photos or videos, and if there is more than one, you should add another heading called "Recommended Videos." Below that heading you will put links to videos you select that can grab students' attention and increase their motivation to do the wiki activities. To find interesting videos, you might go to many of the video websites previously mentioned (e.g., YouTube or TeacherTube, PBS.org, Discovery Channel, Nova Channel, etc.). We do suggest that at this point, you should select shorter rather than longer video segments (again we recommend three- to ten-minute video segments). We also suggest that for each video, you add a few lines denoting the "points to look for" in the video.

Step 5: Add a Navigation Option

At this point, you are well on your way to creating your wiki. However, you will add several additional pages and you need a way to allow students to move from one wiki page to another. Therefore, you need to add a navigation tool to the wiki. In the edit bar at the top of the page is a button called "Wedgets." Click that. A list of options will open, one of which is "Add the Navigation Tool." When you click that, a navigation tool will be added at the bottom of the page to allow you to navigate to other wiki pages.

Step 6: Create Locked and Unlocked Wiki Pages

Now you are nearly finished with the homepage, and you now need to lock up the content that you don't want students to edit. In most cases, teachers don't want the students (or anyone else) to edit the content on the homepage, so that page of content needs to be locked down. While many wiki pages are available for students to edit, the homepage generally should not be.

To lock a page in a wiki, move the cursor to the top right of the edit bar, over the series of dots. Click there. Then you are presented with options, one of which is "Lock" this page. Click that once you are completely done with your homepage. You will need to repeat that lock for each page you want locked down. For others, simply don't perform this step. As creator of the wiki, you will always have the option of unlocking any page for your own edits, so if you wish to change something on the homepage later, you can do so. However, you will need to lock it down at the end of that process.

Step 7: Create Other Wiki Pages

Next, you will need to create additional wiki pages for content that students can edit. These unlocked pages allow students to make contributions to the wiki. One of these should be a vocabulary page. There, teachers should add the vocabulary (but not definitions) of the terms in the unit of instruction. Students can then edit those by providing definitions and examples.

Of course, virtually any activity teachers wish to include may likewise be included as either a locked or unlocked wiki page, and the only real limit is the creativity of the teacher.

Step 8: Adjust the Look and Feel of Your Wiki

As you become a more frequent user of wikispaces, you will learn a wide variety of options to change the color of items or the background color of your wiki. Teachers can use the "Edit This Page" tab in the tool bar at the top of the page to manipulate text, change fonts, and set spacing for each page. You don't need to do this stuff at first, as the wiki will appear normal and you can do a great deal of this just by using various headings, and so on. However, as you become more fluent in using wikis, you will probably begin to experiment with these features and enrich your wikis to make them more engaging for your students.

Step 9: Why Not Add a Webquest?

Virtually any educational content in any form (written content, digital video content, photos, etc.) can be added or linked to your class wiki, so why not include a webquest on one page of the wiki? Once a webquest is developed (see that process described in Tech Tool 2), simply cut and paste that webquest into your class wiki. Even the photos and accompanying videos in the webquest will then be uploaded to your class wiki, and you can add other digital videos simply by clicking on the images file (the icon that looks like a tree in a box).

As this idea suggests, many teachers are now using wikis for subject-area lesson planning and as their class syllabus! Here's an example. When I (the senior author of this text) was initially certified as a secondary social studies teacher, I learned to write a unit-by-unit syllabus for the students. That paper document included:

a two/three week agenda for the unit	*daily activities planned for each day*
all chapter reading assignments	*daily written work assignments for the unit*
assignment due dates	*study guide questions or graphics*
descriptions of unit-length class projects	*any other unit-content activities*

Today, rather than putting all of that on paper in a description of the unit of instruction, teachers are realizing that a wiki is an excellent way to prepare each instructional unit. In this sense, the wiki becomes not only a lesson plan for a single day, but a lesson planning tool for an entire instructional unit. Using wikis in that fashion not only saves paper but makes this information available for both students for work at home, and likewise makes your instructional unit assignments available to parents via the Internet! In short, as you become more fluent in using wikis, you should begin to do much, if not all, of your instructional planning and development within a class wiki. This reflects the best practices for instruction in the 21st century.

Step 10: Invite Students (and Others) to Your Class Wiki

Once your wiki is ready, teachers must invite students to join the wiki using the "User Creator" feature. In some cases, teachers can sign their students up directly, and that is preferable to the invitation process. Generally, we recommend that you begin using a wiki that only students can access. They will be able to edit the unlocked wiki pages, such as the vocabulary page, without disturbing the wiki homepage or other locked content. After using two or three wikis for the class, you will be practiced in the "wiki arts" and you should then invite parents to join the wiki as observers. This can foster a great deal of good will for you and is almost guaranteed to improve the parents' perception of your instructional skills.

In some schools, as a tech-safety option, teachers have chosen to invite administrators, department chairpersons, or other school leaders to likewise join the wiki. This can serve as a useful oversight function if anyone ever raises a question about any of the content on the wiki. While most wiki users don't take this step, it is always available for schools that are just moving into using tech tools and may be advisable under those conditions. Of course, if each of thirty or fifty teachers in a given school is using wikis for all instructional units, this oversight function can become quite a burden. Some schools require teachers to add an administrator to only one wiki per year, to ease that burden. Others do not invite administrators at all unless a problem arises, and again, that is very rare.

How Do I Differentiate With Wikis?

Wikis provide excellent options for differentiating instruction. In fact, any differentiation option you can use in the general education classroom is likewise an option for the wiki. Because wikis allow students to participate in their learning through actual creation of content for the wiki, students will tend to segregate themselves somewhat, based on their learning styles, preferences, and strengths. For example, linguistically talented fifth-grade learners might work individually or together to develop a dialogue for a fictional debate to demonstrate the content of the lesson. For a lesson on World War II as one example, students might develop a debate representing General Patton and Field Marshall Rommel debating the importance of gasoline or ammunition supplies in the North African Campaign of 1942.

However, learners who are more inclined to movement-based learning may wish to develop a month-by-month "walk-through map" of that fluid battle across northern Africa, demonstrating positions of the opposing forces and major events during that fight. This could then be digitally videotaped and uploaded to the class wiki. As an enrichment activity, some of the more advanced fifth-graders could develop a comparison poster that compares that tank battle with the movements of American tanks in the first Iraqi War (which was another battle characterized by fluid, large-scale movements of competing tanks and armor). As these quick examples illustrate, students will have many options to exercise their learning strengths when wikis are offered as a differentiated instructional option.

Conclusions

Wikis are relatively simple to create and use for instruction and provide an excellent way to differentiate instruction. For those reasons, we recommend that all teachers learn to create and use wikis. Not only are wikis good tools for increasing student participation and ultimately academic achievement, they are also excellent for helping students use and understand 21st century technologies. In fact, many wikis are used today in the workplace when individuals from different locales are required to work together, as the editable function of wikis allow the ultimate wiki content to reflect the best thinking of all participants.

> Not only are wikis good tools for increasing student participation and achievement, they are also excellent for helping students use and understand 21st century technologies.

Further, wiki use represents the future (Bender & Waller, 2011). When wikis are used in the classroom, students are not studying content in a passive fashion, such as receiving information from a teacher's lecture or a textbook. Rather, in using wikis students are creating informative content centered around the content under study. In using this teaching tactic, as well as many other 21st century classroom teaching tools, students become much more active in the learning process, and they are practicing skills, such as collaborative thinking and online research, that represent how they will be required to function in the 21st century world (Bender & Waller, 2011).

> In using wikis, students are practicing skills, such as collaborative thinking and online research, that represent how they will be required to function in the 21st century world.

References

Bender, W. N., & Waller, L. (2011). *The teaching revolution: RTI, technology, and differentiation transform teaching for the 21st century.* Thousand Oaks, CA: Corwin.

Richardson, W. (2010). *Blogs, wikis, podcasts, and other powerful tools for educators.* Thousand Oaks, CA: Corwin.

Waller, L. (2011). Is your kid's classroom connection high speed? Six easy ways to engage students with technology in reading! *Teacher's Workshop Newsletter, 4*(1), 1–3.

Watters, A. (2011). *Why wikis still matter.* Retrieved from: http://www.edutopia.org/blog/wiki-classroom-audrey-watters

Part II

Tools for Student Engagement and Empowerment

Tech Tool 5

Cloud Computing

What Do I Need to Know?

It could be argued that virtually any tech tool could increase both student engagement and student empowerment, and Part I presented evidence for enhanced engagement based on providing access, and the use of webquests, wikis, and class blogs. Still, with those initial tech applications explored, there are many exciting and new options for teachers to consider that will enhance student engagement with the subject content; and once C2S2 students become empowered to learn using these 21st century tools, their future learning potential becomes virtually unlimited.

Imagine empowering today's C2S2 students to learn content as independent, self-directed learners! Imagine instructing students on the skills needed to learn from the Internet, in a critical, information evaluation fashion. Imagine teaching every student that anytime, anywhere, digital learning is the learning mode for the future, and that it is the student's individual responsibility to critically evaluate and ultimately master content. Those learners would leave school empowered to learn whatever they needed for the rest of their lives! *Cloud computing* and the next several tools presented below foster that type of engagement with learning content.

We have mentioned previously that C2S2 students are demanding access to their work in various locations, since their personal experience with smartphones has shown them that their virtual social lives (e.g., Facebook and Twitter) are accessible anywhere. Thus, C2S2 students likewise expect the option of doing schoolwork anytime and anywhere. In that regard, one of the most important innovations in teaching today is the onset of cloud-based teaching.

During the 2010 to 2012 time frame, the term *cloud computing* became popular. Cloud computing simply means that rather than house learning software and data on student performance on a single computer at the school, the software as well as student's performance data and individual students' work is housed on servers outside of the school (Richardson & Mancabelli, 2011). While teachers and students would use the same learning programs or educational games in cloud-based teaching as they would for computer-based instruction in the classroom, cloud computing means that those students would have to get online to run those programs. Further, any work they did within that software would be stored, like the software itself, on servers outside the school.

Teaching on the Cloud

> Cloud computing means that rather than house learning software and students' work on a single computer at the school, the software and students' work are housed on a server outside of the school.

While this distinction may sound somewhat trivial, it is not. By using the "cloud," teachers and students can access their software as well as their own work within that software, whenever and wherever they access the Internet. Thus, rather than completing work only at school, students can now get into the same lesson assignment at home, or anywhere else they access the Internet. Thus, this tech-tool option represents freedom to learn content anytime and anywhere.

For example, imagine a fifth-grade student who is working on a PowerPoint presentation on the short story "The Lady or the Tiger." That student may have finished reading the story previously, while she might have completed only a rough outline of the presentation slides and the basic storyboard points for the presentation. Using traditional software, that student would have to wait to return to school the next day to continue that work, since both the software and the student's completed work would be stored on a single computer at school. However, using a program that is cloud-based, she could go home, use a password to get online, and then complete the remaining outline and PowerPoint presentation.

In one sense, cloud computing is not a tool itself, in that it is not hardware (e.g., laptop computers, iPads) or software (such as Voki or some of the tools described later). It is neither an instructional technique (e.g., webquest) nor a website. However, cloud computing does represent a fundamental difference in how instruction can be delivered, and many tools described later in the book are based on cloud computing. For that reason, we wanted to describe this for teachers who might be just beginning their tech journey.

It is a fact that many educational programs today offer this cloud-based option, and the developers of those programs thus provide the computer storage space for schools to use, which saves the costs of those services. In turn, those software companies offer the cloud-server space free in order to sell their programs and software on a fee-per-student basis to the schools.

Open Source Tech Tools

However, with the advent of cloud computing, there is a growing movement to make free software available for teachers and students, including the code used to develop and support the educational software programs. This enables information technology specialists to actually reprogram the software code, and thus modify the software for their particular use. Over the last decade, many educational software companies and developers have chosen to make their software educational programs available for schools at no cost (Richardson & Mancabelli, 2011), and this has come to be called the *open-source movement*. Some developers make an initial level of the software free to schools, whereas they may charge businesses a fee for software use, or they may offer a more extensive level of service to schools that involves payment of a nominal fee. Thus, for some of the tech tools described below, schools may access the software for free, access the underlying code, and also obtain a storage space for student work "on the cloud"! Therefore, the school would pay nothing for both the software and the required computer space for many students to use the software, which can result in large savings for schools in these relatively tough budgetary times. While these issues are typically addressed by the information technology specialists in the school district office, teachers should be aware of these terms, and understand that many educational applications are free or low-cost.

How Would I Differentiate With Cloud-Based Instruction?

The power of cloud-based instruction coupled with open-source software is not merely dependent on individual student access to schoolwork, as illustrated in the example above. Rather, the power of this type of teaching becomes most apparent in small group projects. Imagine that the assignment described above happened to be a group assignment. Not only would one student have access to the work online at home, but all students would have access, opening the door to truly collaborative and highly differentiated work, based on cloud computing. Many students in the small group could access a single assignment based on the cloud and work on that assignment simultaneously at home. Because their work was stored on servers maintained outside the school, the incomplete work would be immediately available online for the entire group.

Further, both cloud-computing and open-source software provide an excellent platform for differentiating instruction, and group projects, in particular, allow students to select their own contributions to the larger group project. That choice, in turn, allows students to select educational endeavors based on their learning style, skill level, and learning preference.

> The power of cloud-based instruction becomes most apparent in small-group projects.

Here is an example of a collaborative small-group, cloud-based project, contrasted with the same type of project from the 1990s. Imagine a seventh-grade teacher teaching science in 1995, focusing on the topic of mammals and reptiles that existed 100,000 years ago. That teacher would probably have differentiated instruction somewhat by identifying several groups of students based on similar interests and learning styles. Next, each group would have been required to develop a research paper on one or two specific animals, perhaps contrasting one reptile and one mammal from that period. Those students would have probably have used encyclopedias, their text, and other resources from the media center to find information, pictures of animals, diagrams, or other data for their report. They would then have written the report, and perhaps shown various pictures to the class when they presented their report.

> Both cloud-computing and open-source software provide an excellent platform for differentiating instruction.

To prepare the written report itself, one student would have done some of the writing, and then hand-delivered those pages to other students for editing. Ultimately, those students would probably have had to recopy or retype that report several times as they moved from the initial draft to the completed paper, prior to handing the assignment in to the teacher and presenting it to the class. Again, that type of small-group research was the model for small-group report writing in the late 20th century classroom.

Now consider the same assignment as a 21st century assignment and housed on the cloud. In a modern cloud-based teaching environment, not only the assignment, but the entire teaching and learning process becomes vastly different, much more collaborative in nature, and generally much more interesting. First, that book report assignment in a 21st century class would not result in merely a hard-copy, written report, but might consist of the production of a wiki on the topic or perhaps an edited, content-rich videotape presentation, such as a student-created podcast. Another option would be a WordPerfect presentation, complete with slides, photos, video clips, all relevant to the topic.

To begin that type of work, one or two students from the group might search the Internet for pictures or brief video segments that illustrate distinctions between mammals and reptiles, while another two or three students in the same group would prepare a video script of information on each animal selected. They would use some type of word processing or document publication function (several of which are described later in this book: see Tech Tool 13— Scribd; Open Office; Tech Tool 15—Google Apps), and thus, the script would not have to be handed from one student to another prior to editing. In fact, any student in the group could help edit that script online, as necessary, with several students working on it at the same time.

> In a modern, cloud-based teaching environment, not only the assignment, but the entire teaching and learning process becomes vastly different, much more collaborative in nature, and generally much more interesting.

Another student might be preparing to digitally record one or two group members delivering a verbal description of each animal, and then that student would digitally overlay those audio-scripted segments with various pictures or video of each animal. By combining these media, the production of the final product becomes much more interesting, and is generally more informative than a written document, and the cloud-based project generally increases both student engagement with the content under study, as well as student collaboration overall.

In that manner, a five- to ten-minute video report or PowerPoint presentation could be developed, housed on the cloud, shown to the class, critiqued by others in the class as well as the teacher, and ultimately published on a school website, a class wiki, or on a worldwide venue, such as YouTube! As educators with years of experience focusing on students' motivational issues, it behooves us to ask, which of these processes is more interesting to students? As this example illustrates, the entire teaching-learning process has become more collaborative in nature and generally much more interesting using cloud computing.

> A book report assignment in a 21st century class would not be a hard-copy, written report, but rather something like the production of a wiki on the topic, or perhaps an edited, content-rich videotape presentation or PowerPoint presentation on the topic.

Further, teachers can clearly see that the 21st century version of the assignment is much better preparation for the types of tasks that students will be expected to do than the 20th century assignment. Indeed, an inability to use these tech-based teaching and learning tools (e.g., wikis, digital media editing, cloud computing, collaborative product development) is likely to handicap students in a manner that no teacher would find acceptable. For this reason, teachers must fully explore these tech-based teaching tools housed on the cloud!

Conclusions

In our discussion of cloud-based teaching, we have not presented explicit steps on "How Do I Get Started?" as we have in virtually every other tech tool in this text. This is because the steps involved differ from one cloud-based tool to another. However, many of the subsequent tech tools described are based on the cloud, and many are open-source tools that are available for educators at no cost. Clearly, using tech tools that are free holds many advantages for schools, and that option, coupled with the BYOD option discussed in the Introduction, removes many of the barriers to tech-based instruction. Once schools have wifi available schoolwide, it is literally true that the sky is the only limit to what can be done in the 21st century classroom!

Reference

Richardson, W., & Mancabelli, R. (2011). *Personal learning networks: Using the power of connections to transform education.* Bloomington, IN: Solution Tree Press.

Tech Tool 6

The Flipped Classroom and Khan Academy

What Do I Need to Know?

Flipped Classrooms

As discussed in the previous section, cloud computing makes the subject-area content, as well as students' individual work, completely accessible at home, and this has led to a fundamentally different method of instruction, the *flipped classroom*. Many teachers are reversing the traditional order of instruction and assigning students to do initial instruction on a brand-new topic as independent study work at home, using video demonstrations and various websites available via cloud-computing options (Cook, 2011; Green, 2012; Maton, 2011). Thus, in a flipped classroom, students are required to use web resources and web-delivered video demonstrations as homework and undertake initial instruction of the lesson content themselves on new topics, while the class time is used for interesting laboratory explorations or practice activities using the new content. In this sense, those teachers have flipped the traditional order of instruction in which a teacher delivers new content via lecture or class discussion and then assigns practice work (typically a work-sheet or report) as homework; initial instruction and homework are *flipped.*

> **Definition:** In a flipped classroom, students are required to use web resources as homework and undertake initial instruction of the lesson content themselves on new topics, while the class time is used for interesting laboratory explorations or practice activities using the new content.

In one recently published example, Green (2012) reported that teachers at Clintondale High School, a financially challenged school in Detroit, flipped their classes. With failure rates "through the roof" in that school, teachers chose to improve student academic performance across the curriculum, so they videotaped their own lectures on new content and posted those videos to the school website. Students were then required to access that content as the initial instructional phase of the lesson when they began a new unit of instruction. The class period then became a laboratory for practice with that content, in which students could request specific help on the content as they practiced and applied that new knowledge.

In this school, the C2S2 students responded quite positively to this flipped-classroom approach, as demonstrated by the data. After eighteen months, Principal Green reported failure rates in the flipped instruction dropped in nearly every subject area: English failure rates dropped from 52 percent to 19 percent, math from 44 percent to 13 percent, science from 41 percent to 19 percent, and social studies from 28 percent to 9 percent. These improvements suggest that flipping the class has positive impact on student achievement across the board, and that indicates that C2S2 students are not only found in affluent districts in which all students own cellphones but in all school districts. Once again, the expectations of today's C2S2 students are demonstrated in these data.

However, with the advent of high-quality, web-based teaching resources and cloud computing, teachers in some subject areas do not have to self-record their instructional content, as many demonstration videos are already available (Edick, 2012). A large number of video demonstrations and instructional examples exist in a wide variety of subject areas, and these videos can be accessed and used by teachers and students alike merely by using open-source websites, such as YouTube and TeacherTube (Edick, 2012). In fact, cloud computing and other innovations in technology make flipped instruction possible, whereas it would have been virtually impossible even five or ten years ago (Sparks, 2011; Toppo, 2011). In addition to the example above, a

> Failure rates in the flipped instruction dropped in nearly every subject area: English failure rates dropped from 52 percent to 19 percent, math from 44 percent to 13 percent, science from 41 percent to 19 percent, and social studies from 28 percent to 9 percent.

great deal of other evidence, some of which is anecdotal in nature, suggests extremely positive results from this flipped-classroom approach to instruction (Cook, 2011; Green, 2012; Maton, 2011; Stansbury, 2012).

Bender (2012) has suggested that the flipped classroom really represents the ultimate example of differentiated instruction, as C2S2 students studying new topics at home alone are very likely to study using their preferred (i.e., their strongest) learning style. Thus, the flipped classroom can be interpreted within the current paradigms of instructional pedagogy. To get a sense of how teachers and students respond to flipping the classroom, a brief video is available on a flipped fifth-grade mathematics class at Lake Elmo Elementary school in Lake Elmo, Minnesota (see the video at http://www.eschoolnews .com/2012/02/09/a-first-hand-look-inside-a-flipped-classroom/). We would urge every teacher to watch that video to get a sense of the excitement associated with flipping the classroom.

Khan Academy!

One tool that has recently bolstered the flipped-classroom movement is the development of the *Khan Academy* (www.khanacademy.org). The Khan Academy is a free online mathematics, chemistry, and physics curriculum (with some content in other areas) that is housed on the cloud, and represents anytime-anywhere learning. It was developed by Mr. Sal Khan and structured as a nonprofit organization; it is completely free for anyone to use, worldwide! The curriculum exercises range across grade levels from kindergarten up though high school and into college. While most of the focus has been in

Figure 6.1

Source: © 2012 Khan Academy

mathematics, curriculum content ranges across many subject areas, and is constantly expanding in areas, such as history, astronomy, personal finance, biology, and earth sciences.

> **Definition:** The Khan Academy is a free online mathematics, chemistry, and physics curriculum (with some content in other areas) that is housed on the cloud, and represents anytime-anywhere learning.

Because the Khan Academy is a cloud-based, it represents an anytime-anywhere learning tool for C2S2 kids worldwide (Sparks, 2011; Toppo, 2011; Watters, 2011). It is self-directed such that C2S2 kids can study this curricular content alone, but many teachers from Grade 1 and up are beginning to use Khan Academy in some fashion in their classrooms. Khan Academy has received significant funding from the Bill and Melinda Gates Foundation, Google, and other foundations over the years, to ramp up their service capabilities and make this available at no cost to students and teachers worldwide. While many curriculum areas are now included, the Khan Academy content was originally focused more heavily in mathematics, so we'll use examples from that curricular area below.

The website presents three major components of this program: game-based exercises, video demonstrations, and an individual knowledge map. First, there are thousands of online learning exercises and game-based activities in mathematics, physics, and chemistry as well as some academic content in other areas. Next, the website presents video demonstrations of how to do many of the specific types of problems or exercises. In those videos, students see an interactive whiteboard where the various steps of the problem appear, as a "voice" guides the students through the problem by explaining the necessary steps. For example, Level 1 linear equations such as $4X + 6 = 22$ are presented, and multiple steps are shown on the board as students are guided toward the solution to the problem. While the steps are discussed, the narrator explains the reasons for various steps and mathematics operations. Thus, this curriculum can function, for many students, as initial instruction on that type of mathematics problem!

Generally, students will access the website, try some practice exercises, and then if necessary, watch a demonstration video on one particular type of problem (Toppo, 2011; Watters, 2011). Throughout the exercises, students are highly motivated by the gaming basis of this curricular support program, but the program also provides the opportunity to earn badges, which are displayed on each student's knowledge map, to show that student's own progress. As soon as students begin their work, they will begin to earn these badges and points for learning specific content. The more students challenge themselves, the more they achieve, and the more badges they earn—thus the more bragging rights they get! While some badges can be earned by successful completion of one or two exercises, other badges take many months or even years to earn. Over 3,200 videos are included that present demonstrations of particular problems on which students might need help, and more are added each month. Each video is a single chunk of topical information and is not over ten minutes in length.

Finally, each student is provided with an individual knowledge map. The *Knowledge Maps* are individual progress monitoring tools that track each student's progress in relation to the whole curriculum. Anecdotal evidence suggests that students typically find the knowledge map quite motivating. Students (or their coaches) can determine from the knowledge map what the student has completed, what concepts have been mastered, and what the student's next emphasis needs to be. The knowledge map will also remind students when they might need a review of certain content. It is not an overstatement to say that the knowledge map, as both a progress-tracking and motivational tool, is the core of this program for individual students.

However, other documentation is also available for teachers with Khan Academy. For example, a class profile lets teachers glance at the dashboard, which is a classwide summary of performance. Teachers can then determine what content to emphasize in the math lab (or the other subject areas) the following day. Also, students' performance data are presented as an X/Y axis chart showing individual student growth over time. Using these documentation tools, teachers or parents will know immediately if a particular student is having difficulty with any particular content, and they can then assign other videos on that content or work through a video with the student. Further, all of these data are saved over time so that teachers can review students' progress and make determinations about students' rates of progress relative to stated goals.

> The Knowledge Map within Khan Academy is an individualized student progress-monitoring tool that tracks each individual student's progress in relation to the whole curriculum.

While we are strong advocates of Khan Academy for virtually all teachers in mathematics across the grade levels, we do wish to note a couple of criticisms of this program that we consider valid. First, while the gaming aspect of this tech tool is highly motivational, the videos may be somewhat less compelling.

Specifically, in many of the video demonstrations, the student sees a mathematics problem being completed on an interactive whiteboard, while a disembodied "teacher's" voice discusses the steps to follow to solve the problem. In one sense, that represents an excellent example of 19th century teaching—seeing a math problem done on the board while a teacher describes the steps.

Another concern is the level of the explanations in the videos. These step-by-step descriptions are basically directed at normally achieving students. Of course, that is exactly as it should be, given the overall goals of anytime-anywhere learning that are the basis for Khan Academy. However, these step-by-step instructions may be aimed at a level that is slightly too high for some students with learning challenges. Specifically, students with intellectual disabilities or learning disabilities may need a more in-depth, one-to-one instruction from the teacher to understand the step-by-step process for a given type of mathematics problem.

Still, even with these problems noted, we do recommend that every teacher who is teaching mathematics investigate the use of Khan Academy and consider flipping the instruction in class. Here are some specific steps we recommend to help you begin.

How Do I Get Started Using the Flipped Classroom and the Khan Academy?

The first step in using Khan Academy and flipping your classroom is to become very familiar with the Khan Academy. The Khan Academy website presents many tools for coaches (i.e., teachers, mentors, or parents) to use as they guide students through Khan Academy learning experiences. The website features specific exercises for virtually any type of mathematics problem that might be covered in the Common Core State Standards, ranging from one-plus-one up through calculus, though there has been no particular effort to relate these exercises to the Common Core State Standards, as Khan Academy is intended as anytime-anywhere learning for students worldwide.

Working at home, students then use the gaming feature to practice that particular type of problem. Each problem in the game-based practice sessions can be broken down into simple step-by-step instructions provided as immediate feedback should any student experience difficulty with a particular type of problem. Several guidelines on how to begin using the Khan Academy have emerged from teachers who are actually using this in their classes, and these are presented here.

Step 1: Explore Khan Academy

Prior to using this in the classroom, teachers should explore Khan Academy content themselves, just as they would any new teaching curriculum or approach. Take care to investigate the fit between Khan Academy coverage of content and terminology and the terminology used in your curriculum. Also consider the knowledge map and possible use of that in your class.

Step 2: Get Signed In

Consider your school's Internet usage policies and make certain your administrators are kept in the loop relative to your use of this resource. Also, carefully investigate how teachers sign students into Khan Academy. Ultimately teachers should register their entire class, including students who have no computer or Internet access at home.

Step 3: Use This Tool in Class First

While Khan Academy is structured as a stand-alone teaching tool, having students access and use it in the classroom is recommended, since teachers can troubleshoot any access issues with their students. Teachers generally indicate that they find it beneficial to teach students how to use this resource prior to flipping the class, and many use Khan Academy as a reference tool to supplement class activities at first, until students get used to it. For example, at Hapeville Charter Middle School in Atlanta, Georgia, the mathematics faculty began using Khan Academy videos as demonstration tools. When students asked a question on a mathematics process, several teachers began by referring them to Khan Academy for a demonstration of the math problem. Once the students went through one or several of the videos, those students could explain that mathematical process to the class. Viewing these videos is also a great partner activity in class.

Step 4: BYOD

Encourage students to BYOD (bring your own device) for Internet access.

After discussing the issue with your administrators, teachers should not wait for schools to purchase laptops or iPads for students—have students BYOD! All that is needed is Internet capability. One long-term goal is to get students used to seeking information on the Internet and using that information to solve problems in mathematics or answer questions in other subject areas. Students should emerge from schools as independent, self-directed learners, and this teaching tool can be used to foster those skills.

Step 5: Share Khan Academy With Parents

In general, it is always a good idea to keep parents in the loop, and teachers should let parents know of Khan Academy. Parental permission would not typically be necessary, but providing parents with this information is advisable for several reasons. One reason that some parents are reluctant to assist or even monitor their child's homework is that they may not know the content, and they don't want their child to view them as uneducated. With Khan Academy, that worry can be alleviated, as the videos can be used by child and parent together while working through a problem.

In some cases reported to these authors, parents have used Khan Academy to learn content that was not related to their child's curriculum. For example, one teacher reported looking at the Khan Academy information on personal finance when considering the purchase of a home! Another teacher reported that he was using Khan Academy to assist his own child in algebra, since his background in that subject was not strong. It is clear from anecdotal reports that Khan Academy opens many doors for parents and child to work together on schoolwork, but this is much more likely when the teacher, using Khan Academy, encourages it. Sending a letter or e-mail home about this curriculum and suggesting that parents and students work through this together can often get parents involved in the process.

> Some parents and teachers have used Khan Academy to learn content that was not related to their child's curriculum.

Step 6: Use the Knowledge Map

The Knowledge Map within Khan Academy is an organizational tool to let students and their parents know what the students should study next. As students demonstrate their ability in certain content, the knowledge map awards them a badge and then suggests the next area for them to study. As reported in the literature of flipped classrooms, this empowers students, and some have moved far beyond their own grade placement in various subject areas (Green, 2012;

Toppo, 2011). Clearly, earning these badges is quite motivating for some. For students who do excel, additional classroom or schoolwide recognition is always recommended!

Step 7: Assign as a Preinstructional Assignment

At some point, after students have demonstrated their ability to use Khan Academy in the classroom, you should begin to assign homework in the curriculum. Of course, many students can begin with Khan Academy with no in-class practice (indeed, it is intended to be used in that fashion), but others will need some help initially. However, teachers should move all students in the direction of using Khan Academy content as a stand-alone learning tool.

Step 8: Record the Content

If you are trying a flipped lesson based on self-recorded content or other web-based content (again, both YouTube and TeacherTube are excellent options for finding specific instructional content, Edick, 2012), you will need to record the information students are to learn. Generally shorter videos, rather than hour-long lectures, are recommended. These do not have to be "professionally" done, but they should present a chunk of information with adequate sound and video demonstrations if possible. Using pictures from the text or other resources from the web can make these brief recorded pieces of information more interesting as well as more informative.

Step 9: Require Note-Taking

Some teachers have chosen to have students make notes on the Khan Academy content, or other video-recorded content, as they practice a particular problem or watch a demo video at home (Cook, 2011; Sparks, 2011; Toppo, 2011). Note-taking is a skill that will well serve students throughout life, as they become lifelong learners, and if students are viewing recorded content other than Khan Academy, note-taking is the only means by which a teacher can check their understanding of that content. Thus, in flipped classrooms based on teacher-delivered, recorded content, note-taking is critical. Teachers should check those notes, since in such a procedure, teachers get a good sense of who accomplished what the night before. Ultimately, note-checking will tell who did their assigned work in studying the new content, and thus, requiring note-taking is recommended both within the context of Khan Academy and for other web-based learning as well.

Step 10: Try a Flipped Lesson

Once students are used to using Khan Academy content or other video demonstrations of the content in the above fashion, your class is ready to try the "flip!" Even if some reluctant students are still having difficulty in the curriculum, teachers can assign content as a homework assignment that has not been taught at all in class and then conduct the following class as a project-oriented class, a drill and practice game for students, or a math-lab type of class.

> Note-taking and note-checking will tell who did their assigned work in Khan Academy at home and who did not.

Each teacher's ultimate goal should be instilling in all students the belief that they can seek out, find, and master difficult academic content on their own, with no teacher to teach them. This is truly the goal of anytime-anywhere learning and should be a primary focus of all educational endeavors.

How Do I Differentiate Using the Flipped Classroom and the Khan Academy?

If differentiated instruction is best understood as students using their preferred learning styles and preferences to master difficult content, then the essence of differentiated instruction is instruction in which students independently choose how to learn. Of course, individualized, computer-based learning facilitates such differentiated instructional choices as well as any learning approach. Thus, flipped classes work to effectively differentiate instruction both with Khan Academy and without.

However, within the Khan Academy curriculum, teachers are encouraged to set up student accounts for every student in the class. Students' work in the curriculum is saved on their individual knowledge map, which teachers, students, and parents can access. Teachers can then see the data on each student's progress, and this fosters further differentiation, as teachers review what individual students have mastered.

Other Online, Broad-Scale Curricula

While Khan Academy has, understandably, generated a great deal of media attention, there are many online curricula that can provide teachers with excellent supportive instructional materials, and any of these might well provide the option of flipping the classroom as discussed above. One large-scale, online curriculum that is being used increasingly in schools is the SAS Curriculum Pathways (sascurriculumpathways.com). This site provides extensive free online curricula with materials and instructional activities in English, language arts, science, social studies, mathematics, and Spanish. The lesson activities are designed around the Common Core State Standards and are appropriate for Grades 6 through 12. While the curriculum is free, teachers are required to log in to access the material, and a brief tutorial video is available free of charge at the website above. The company behind this website designed the curriculum materials extremely carefully, with content experts in various subject areas consulting on all aspects of the curriculum. This is a free option that we encourage all teachers in those grade levels to consider.

Another example that includes curriculum materials for students in lower grades is BrainPOP (www.brainpop.com). BrainPOP is a fee-based site and uses animated characters to teach curriculum-based content in a variety of areas, including math, science, social studies, English, technology, arts and music, and health. The site includes a free, short tutorial video as well as extensive movies, quizzes, experiments, timelines, and activities. The content is aligned to and searchable by state standards but not by Common Core standards (as of February, 2012). These instructional activities are appropriate and recommended for Grades 3 and up.

Conclusions: Game Changers in Education!

As the discussion above suggests, a number of online curricula in a variety of subject areas are available today. However, even with this plethora of curricula available, the flipped classroom and the Khan Academy concept that is largely associated with it can accurately be considered "game changers" in education! Both represent empowering students to effectively use multiple sources for anytime-anywhere learning that is student driven. This is learning for the future, and these tools have only become available within the last decade. With Khan Academy, students worldwide are now free to seek and master nearly any content they choose, and this can be truly empowering. Teaching students to seek information, evaluate it, and apply it will ultimately lead to highly capable, lifelong learners, a worthy goal indeed for all educators. This may very well be the single most important of the 21st century tech tools now available, and we do recommend that every teacher, and in particular every teacher of mathematics, explore this powerful, free tech tool.

References

Bender, W. N. (2012). *The new differentiated instruction for students with learning disabilities: Teaching for the 21st century.* Thousand Oaks, CA: Corwin.

Cook, G. (2011). *A compelling way to teach math—"flipping" the classroom.* Retrieved from http://articles.boston.com/2011/09/18/bostonglobe/30172469_1_math-khan-academy-high-tech-education

Edick, H. (2012). *8 crucial resources for flipped classrooms.* Retrieved from http://edudemic.com/2012/03/8-crucial-resources-for-flipped-classrooms/

Green, G. (2012). *Flipped classrooms give every student a chance to succeed!* Retrieved from http://schoolsofthought.blogs.cnn.com/2012/01/18/my-view-flipped-classrooms-give-every-student-a-chance-to-succeed/?htp=hp_bn1

Maton, N. (2011). *Can an online game crack the code to language learning?* Retrieved from http://mindshift.kqed.org/2011/11/can-an-online-game-crack-the-code-to-language-learning/

Sparks, S. D. (2011). Schools "flip" for lesson model promoted by Khan Academy. *Education Today, 31*(5), 1–14.

Stansbury, M. (2012). A first-hand look inside a flipped classroom. *eSchool News.* Retrieved from http://www.eschoolnews.com/2012/02/09/a-first-hand-look-inside-a-flipped-classroom/

Toppo, G. (2011, October 6). "Flipped" classrooms take advantage of technology. *USA Today.* Retrieved from http://www.usatoday.com/news/education/story/2011-10-06

Watters, A. (2011). *Khan Academy expands to art history, Sal Khan no longer its only faculty member.* Retrieved from http://www.hackeducation.com/2011/10/19/Khan-academy-expands-to-art-history-sal-khan-no-longer-its-only-faculty-member

Tech Tool 7

Wiffiti

What Do I Need to Know?

Have you ever wanted to know what students were thinking during an instructional lesson or a class discussion? Most teachers at one point or another in their career have wondered how well students understood initial instruction. *Wiffiti* is a new tech tool that is simple to use and will display students' answers to reflective questions during the lesson itself, and that can help teachers get an accurate sense of how well students are following along during any phase of instruction. Wiffiti.com (a combination of Wi-Fi and graffiti) is a website that publishes user messages (in this case, student messages) to a large screen for viewing in the classroom. Essentially, a Wiffiti user (the student) sends messages to the teacher at the Wiffiti site via a mobile device or personal computer and the message is displayed for the entire class or other large audience.

> **Definition:** Wiffiti is a new tech tool that is simple to use and will display students' answers to reflective questions during the lesson itself, and that can help teachers get an accurate sense of how well students are following along during any phase of instruction.

In the public arena, Wiffiti is often used at sporting events on jumbotrons or at large conferences on televisions posted around the meeting room. Wiffiti has made appearances at the Republican and Democratic National Conventions, at concerts, and gallery openings (Staino, 2012). Of course, Wiffiti has applicable uses in the education world as well. Imagine asking a question during your class and allowing students to use the text messaging feature on their cell phone to send their answer in to your interactive whiteboard. In essence, you have an empty bulletin board, and students are able to write on that bulletin board using their mobile device or computer. Their responses are instantaneously published for their peers and for you to view and analyze (Staino, 2010).

This public sharing of ideas is becoming more and more important for our learners, and publishing one-sentence answers to questions can increase engagement with the question at hand, which in turn will make any class much more interesting. According to Pew Research, the availability of social networking and mobile computing has created a new type of student—one that is eager to collaborate and one that relies heavily on feedback from peers (Waters, 2011). The use of Wiffiti in the classroom will accommodate these student-led demands and invigorate class discussions in any subject area.

> Public sharing of ideas is becoming more and more important for our learners, and publishing one-sentence answers to questions can increase engagement with the question at hand, which in turn will make any class much more interesting.

Wiffiti is providing teachers with a forum for instantaneous feedback that can be seen by every student in the room (mrkaiser208, 2010). Using Wiffiti embraces technology, such as text messaging, that students are already using on a daily basis. Research suggests that more than half of children from ages five to eight have used a mobile device, such as a smartphone or iPod ("How to Teach," 2011), and teachers must embrace the technology that our learners see as standard in order to teach these young students in the digital age. It cannot be overstated that offering high levels of student-to-student interaction will engage students more fully in the content material (Bender & Waller, 2011; Richtel, 2012).

Using basic instructions below and on the Wiffiti homepage, teachers can easily create Wiffiti question screens, and once a screen is created, Wiffiti.com will publish a code at the top instructing your students on how they should text in their responses to your question. Again, if students do not have cell phones or mobile devices with Internet capability, they can use their personal computer to log onto the Wiffiti screen and type in their message.

All messages displayed on the Wiffiti screen are anonymous, which encourages shy students to participate a bit more. Once students send in a

Figure 7.1

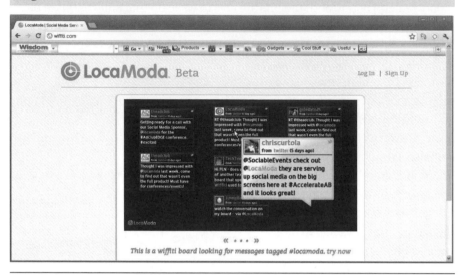

Source: © 2012 LocaModa Inc.

message, Wiffiti.com replies to their phone with a text message that tells them what their username is. Students will be able to identify their message on the board by locating their username, but it will remain anonymous to their peers. This is extremely helpful for those students reluctant to share their ideas or opinions in class, as it provides a forum for intimidation-free sharing of ideas. As messages come in, they continually move around on the screen so that all messages are seen on a loop, and all eventually receive equal prominence.

How Do I Get Started Using Wiffiti?

> All messages displayed on the Wiffiti screen are anonymous, which encourages shy students to participate a bit more.

Step 1: Create a Wiffiti Account

The first thing you need to do to get started is go to www.wiffiti.com and sign up for a free account. This simply involves creating a username, providing your e-mail and mobile phone number, and creating a password for your use.

Step 2: Set Up a Wiffiti Screen

Once you are signed up, creating your first Wiffiti screen is easy. Simply go to the tab labeled "Make a screen." Once there you will see a four-step process on the left of your computer screen. You will need to add tags that describe what your screen will be about. If you are creating a screen so that your students can respond to an in-class discussion on the Civil War, you might add tags including Civil War, North, South, and Battles. You will then need to choose your message sources. While you may receive messages from a variety of sources, we suggest that you select text messaging for classroom use. Specifically, we do not recommend choosing the Twitter option within Wiffiti, as that will bring in messages from the Twitter site that contain any of your tags and are not from your students.

Step 3: Choose Content for Your Question

The third step, choosing content material, is very important for teachers in helping ensure appropriate use of the technology tool. Be sure you click on the option that only allows G-rated messages to appear on your screen. Finally, you can upload a background to make the screen more thematic. Going back to the Civil War example, you may choose a piece of clip art showing a soldier or a battlefield. A background is not necessary or required, but it does add a visual element to the discussion. Finally, you will need to give your screen a title and click the publish screen option.

Step 4: Display the Wiffiti Screen for the Class

Once the screen has been published, you can display it on your interactive whiteboard or other classroom display devices (e.g., LED projector and screen). At the top of the screen, a code will appear that tells students how to text in their response. If a student does not have a mobile device, he can log onto the Wiffiti.com website and in the search box type in the title of your created screen. From there he can post his own response and it will appear just like the text messages that are sent in.

Step 5: Keep Up With Wiffiti Changes

Like all tech tools, Wiffiti is likely to change over time. In fact, according to the Wiffiti.com website, a newer version of Wiffiti will be available by 2013.

This new Wiffiti site will certainly be improved for teachers, as it promises to offer the ability to make screens private as opposed to screens being available for anyone who searches for them on the web. Wiffiti also is developing new moderation tools that will allow teachers to preview and approve student posts. These features will certainly enhance the use of Wiffiti in the classroom, though we recommend that you experiment with Wiffiti now and not wait for these innovations. Teachers can protect students from inappropriate postings by reviewing the school's acceptable use policy, and developing consequences for any inappropriate messaging. Finally, we also recommend deleting the screens after they have been used in the classroom as way to keep them from being stored in the public archive.

How Do I Differentiate With Wiffiti?

Although Wiffiti should be viewed as more of a brainstorming tool during initial instruction and class discussions, it can also function as an avenue for differentiation in the classroom. This tool gives the students the opportunity to anonymously send in their own ideas for assignments, projects, and papers, and shy students or academically-challenged students can comfortably post their thoughts without embarrassment; ultimately this will increase class participation.

> Wiffiti should be viewed as more of a brainstorming tool during initial instruction and class discussions, but it can also function as an avenue for differentiation in the classroom.

Imagine teaching a class on Shakespearean literature. At the end of the unit, you give students the option to send in their messages regarding how they would like to demonstrate their understanding of the content. Students may send in ideas, such as write an essay, re-enact a scene, and create an illustration of the plot line, and each of those is suggestive of different learning styles. Teachers can then determine which options might be appropriate for demonstrating knowledge of that content. Further, teachers would then have the ability to look at the students' goals, ideas, and suggestions when planning the assessment portion of the instructional unit. This gives students a voice in the process while also allowing you to see the types of assessments that students are motivated to complete. When you approve two or three ideas for the final assessment, you have differentiated the product portion of your unit in a way that accommodates various learning styles in your classroom.

Wiffiti clearly encourages learners to be more involved in the presentation process. When you are introducing new content material, learners can use the Wiffiti board to text in questions or concerns relating to the material. Again, in an anonymous fashion, students are able to voice their own issues pertaining to new content. This instantaneous feedback during the presentation of new content helps you tailor your instruction. Instead of waiting for data from later assessment, you can now glance at the Wiffiti board and immediately address the varying needs of your students.

When using Wiffiti, you may have students texting in questions that encourage you to go deeper with the material. You may then either choose to address those during the presentation or to address a small group of students after the presentation with more challenging material. You may

> Wiffiti clearly encourages learners to be more involved in the presentation process.

also find that a small group of students are texting in responses that indicate a need for further intervention. You can use that information to create a small intervention group after the lesson. Wiffiti helps you differentiate by providing instantaneous feedback that helps drive instruction in your classroom.

A Sample Wiffiti Lesson Plan

Standard: North Carolina Standard Course of Study for Social Studies in Eighth Grade

Goal 2.02

Describe the contributions of key North Carolina and national personalities from the Revolutionary War era and assess their influence on the outcome of the war. (While we realized that many states are moving into the Common Core State Standards, other states are not. Some states will use a combination of state standards and the Common Core State Standards. Therefore we have used standards from the Common Core and various states in this book.)

Students will . . .

- Be able to use technology as a means for demonstrating understanding
- Be able to describe the contributions of national personalities from the Revolutionary War era and assess their influence on the outcome of the war
- Be able to summarize the thoughts of various national personalities in deciding whether or not to declare war on Great Britain

Materials

- Mobile device with Internet capabilities or personal computer with Internet access
- Interactive whiteboard

Preparation

- Create a Wiffiti.com account if not previously created
- Create a Wiffiti screen entitled "Thoughts on Declaring War"

Directions

- Prior to beginning the lesson, the teacher will again reiterate the appropriate use policy of the school when using mobile devices and Internet capabilities in the classroom.
- Review past content material on several key personalities in the Continental Congress. Discuss those who were for and against declaring war on Great Britain.
- Have students work in pairs and choose one personality. Using the text message feature on their mobile device (or their personal computer), students must create a succinct response depicting their stance on declaring war. Once the response is created, students will send their answer to the Wiffiti board.
- Since the messages will be displayed anonymously, have classmates read each response and determine which personality is represented.
- Have students continue the lesson by using the Wiffiti board as a debate platform. Through text messages, let students continue assuming the opinion of their chosen national personality and text in their argument for or against the war. At the end of the session, have the class vote on the most convincing argument. If it was up to this Wiffiti board, would they have gone to war?

Conclusions

Wiffiti is a simple tool that teachers can use to make their instruction seem much more modern. While this tool will not dramatically change the learning processes in the classroom, it can serve to engage C2S2 students a bit more during whole group lessons. Further, this tool will help teachers gain insight into students' thoughts and understanding during class discussions. For teachers who use whole group discussion frequently, we do recommend this tech tool.

References

Bender, W., & Waller, L. (2011). *The teaching revolution: RTI, technology, and differentiation transform teaching for the 21st century.* Thousand Oaks, CA: Corwin.

How to teach young children in the digital age. (2011, November 9). *eClassroom News.* Retrieved from http://www.eclassroomnews.com/2011/11/09/how-to-teach-young-children-in-the-digital-age/?

mrkaiser208. (2010, March 20). Five ways to teach with Wiffiti in the classroom. *Web 2.0: Enhancing education with technology.* Retrieved from http://web20edu.com/2010/03/20/five-ways-to-teach-with-wiffiti-in-the-classroom/

Richtel, M. (2012, January 20). Blogs vs. term papers. *New York Times.* Retrieved from http://www.nytimes.com/2012/01/22/education/edlife/muscling-in-on-the-term-paper-tradition.html?_r=1

Staino, R. (2010, April 4). Cell phones in the classroom? Wiffiti says yes. *School Library Journal.* Retrieved from http://www.schoollibraryjournal.com/article/CA6727431.html

Waters, J. (2011, December 13). Broadband, social networks, and mobility have spawned a new kind of learner. *The Journal.* Retrieved from http://thejournal.com/Articles/2011/12/13/Broadband-Social-Networks-and-Mobility.aspx?Page=1

Tech Tool 8

Jing

 ## What Do I Need to Know?

In the 21st century classroom, video and visual images will play an increasing role since students today are used to learning via video, pictures, animation, high quality graphics, and other images. For that reason, teachers must learn to capture videos and other images for instructional purposes, and then manipulate them, explain them, add notes to them, and create teaching tools based on the images. As discussed in Tech Tool 6, "The Flipped Classroom and the Khan Academy," teachers are using video demonstrations in the classroom with remarkable success, and tools that facilitate the use and manipulation of images can also result in increased student engagement and empowerment.

Jing is one such image manipulation tool. Jing is free downloadable software that allows teachers to capture video and images that are available on the computer screen and share those images or videos instantly in class. Once the program is downloaded, a sun icon will be visible at the top of your computer screen. When you have an image on your screen that you want to capture, simply click on the sun and highlight the window, pane, or region of your screen you want to save. Once the image is captured, you can add in text boxes, arrows, highlights, and captions, which will greatly enhance the efficacy of the image for teaching. For example, when a picture is presented using Jing, teachers can add notations pointing out the aspects of the image that suggest the major points emphasized within the instructional unit, and those notes become available throughout the unit for the students.

Definition: Jing is free downloadable software that allows teachers to capture video and images that are available on the computer screen and share those images or videos instantly in class.

If you have a video, a series of slides, or other teaching process you want to capture, you may use the sun icon to video that section of the computer screen. All you need to do is highlight the area on your computer screen that you wish to capture and anything that happens in that section of your screen will be a part of the video. Your mouse movements and voice-overs will walk the observer through the video or demonstration process shown on the screen. These videos can be up to five minutes in length. Once you have created an image or video you would like to share, it can be instantly uploaded to Twitter, Facebook, the class wiki, or a blog, or simply shared via e-mail.

Jing is a newer technology tool for teachers so the possibilities of how to incorporate it into the classroom are still being discovered. This tool is likewise being used in business; for example, TechSmith Corporation started Jing in 2007 as a mode of communication with employees, and many other companies are getting creative with its various uses. Most applications in the educational arena are centered on helping teachers and students communicate.

Using video and audio with students makes learning concise and can extend learning past the school day. Here is one example. Many teachers are using Jing to evaluate student work and provide immediate feedback on assignments. In one instance, a high school English teacher took a snapshot of her computer screen while the students' essay papers were being presented on the screen (TechSmith, 2012). She then created for each student a personal Jing video, walking the student through the strengths and weaknesses of the paper. The students thus saw their paper on the video and followed the teacher's voice as she highlighted various issues and clicked on particular parts of the paper. This type of immediate feedback can be essential for many students, and will greatly increase the impact of learning.

As another example, a math teacher might use Jing to capture short videos of problems that are reviewed in class (TechSmith, 2012). In that instance, students would be able to go onto the teacher's website and choose the video that they need to watch, as discussed in the flipped classroom section (see Tech Tool 6). The videos will walk students through the problem while the audio explains the concepts. Instead of having to wait until the next day to get help with those problems, students are receiving extra intervention on their time, for their needs, exactly when they need it.

Perhaps the biggest advantage of this tool is that Jing encourages communication. Using Jing, a teacher can communicate with students about their work in a private virtual conference and can provide specific intervention strategies without embarrassing students in class. Jing also provides an opportunity for students

> A math teacher might use Jing to capture short videos of problems that are reviewed in class.

to work closely with their peers. Students can post their own work to a class blog and record additional information for their peers. Peers can then watch the video and provide constructive criticism for improvement. Thus, Jing will increase student engagement and provide options for students to engage in content conversations well past the end of the school day. Like many tech tools, Jing is a teaching tool that excites and motivates students.

How Do I Get Started Using Jing?

Step 1: Download Jing

To get started using Jing in your classroom, visit the website and click on the free download application (http://www.techsmith.com/download/jing/default .asp). You will then follow the download wizard to successfully install the program onto your computer. Once the program is installed, a sun icon will appear at the top of your desktop, and that sun icon is the control center for Jing.

Step 2: Capture Images for Instruction

As an example, imagine you are teaching an elementary class on insect body parts. You have chosen an insect image from any source on the web, and that image is on your computer screen. To capture the image, put your mouse over the sun icon and click on the crosshairs. Drag the crosshairs so that they outline the portion of the image you wish to utilize in the classroom. Once you have the image highlighted, look at the toolbar toward the bottom of your screen and click "Capture Image."

Step 3: Edit the Image

At that point, you have captured the image, and you will see that image appear in a box for editing. During that editing process, you can add arrows and text boxes to label your insect diagram so that your labels are consistent with the terminology in your curriculum. You may also insert notes for students to observe detailed parts of the insect body.

Step 4: Capture and Edit Videos

This user-friendly process varies only slightly should you wish to capture video from the computer. Again you will begin at the sun icon and click on the crosshairs button. This allows you to select the portion of your computer screen that you want to capture. Once you have selected the appropriate section of your screen, go to the Jing tool bar at the bottom left and select "Capture Video." A countdown will appear and then the recording begins. Any action that you make on your computer screen will be recorded, and the audio feature allows you to explain the process. If you do not want to record audio, you can select the "Mute" button on the Jing toolbar. You can also pause the recording so that you can open new files, open a different document, or change what is on the screen. When you are finished recording, simply click "Stop" and a Jing window will open that allows you to preview your video. If you are satisfied with your recording, save your video or share it via Twitter, Facebook, or other communication tool. Selecting "Save on screencast.com" will provide you a link that is easily shared via e-mail, wikis, or blogs.

How Do I Differentiate With Jing?

Jing is a tool that makes differentiation so much easier because, using Jing, you are able to create personalized intervention and enrichment videos for individual students or groups of students with similar learning styles and preferences. If you have a class wiki or blog, you can use the links from your Jing videos and image captures to store tutorial sessions for students. You can video yourself reteaching a particular problem or lesson and store that on your class wiki and that video will be useful the following year for the same content! When a student needs further help with that content material, she can go online and view the video privately at home or at school. This availability of immediate intervention helps keep students from getting too frustrated while trying to work independently at home or even at school, and it empowers students to learn content anytime and anywhere. Teachers can even recommend to parents that the parents review the video demonstrations with their students at home! Using and storing these videos and images provides a bank of review videos and demonstration material for students to use during exams or prior to state testing.

However, differentiated instruction is not exclusively about interventions and help for students who may be struggling in particular content areas.

Differentiation is also about providing extra enrichment for those students who are excelling in content areas and need goals that challenge their ability level. Jing provides an avenue for this as well. Teachers can use Jing to create videos and help students solve problems that are more challenging than the grade-level text might present. Thus, advanced students can work to solve these problems at home or as an extra in-class assignment. Teachers can also use the Jing capture tools to show students how these problems are applicable in the work world, while having advanced students work through highly challenging application problems.

Students needing extra challenge can also be tasked with creating intervention videos using Jing. Have these students practice explaining the *why* behind particular problems and use their tutorials as part of the online catalogue of demonstration videos intended to help other students. This form of peer tutoring can be used as an innovative instructional strategy for Tier 1, Tier 2, or Tier 3 instruction during the response-to-intervention process (see Bender & Waller, 2011, for more on the Response To Intervention Initiative). This type of peer interaction also promotes collaboration between students with varying academic levels and encourages them to work through new content or review and practice skills that need extra attention (Bender & Waller, 2011). Again, students enjoy the social aspect of learning that these new tech tools can provide, and this type of peer tutoring works because these tools increase student enjoyment and their on-task time, as they discuss academic content (Bender & Waller, 2011).

Creating various styles of videos also helps address the varying learning styles that may be evident in your classroom. Students may need to see several types of problems solved in order to fully grasp new content material and Jing provides you with the time outside of class to explore extra explanations or examples of various problems. It also provides time for you to show various methods for solving different content problems. If you know that a particular student uses mnemonic devices to remember important dates and sequences, you may wish to record a Jing video for your class wiki that highlights those devices. If a particular student needs to see an image, you can capture various images that correlate with the content material and have those readily available. Jing's most beneficial learning application is that it allows you to create instructional tools that can be accessed at any time of the day; ultimately students always have access to your instruction and content matter.

Conclusions

Collaboration is strongly encouraged in the development of teaching paradigms for 21st century classrooms. Teachers are encouraged to envision classrooms that are developed around collaboration—collaboration between the student and teacher and collaboration among the students themselves

(McCrea, 2012). While the possible uses of this tool are only today being explored, it is clear that Jing is the perfect medium to produce this type of collaboration, as students or teachers can video capture content for students. The communication options are endless.

A Sample Lesson Plan

Standard: North Carolina Standard Course of Study for Mathematics in Fifth Grade
   Goal 4.01 and 4.02
   The learner will understand and use graphs and data analysis to collect, organize, analyze, and display data (including stem-and-leaf plots) to solve problems. The learner will compare and contrast different representations of the same data and discuss the effectiveness of each representation.

Students will . . .

- Be able to collect data from peers
- Create two different graphs on their computer
- Use Jing video capture technology to explain their graphical representation of the data

Materials

- Computer access
- Internet access

Preparation

- Download Jing onto each student computer.
- Put students in pairs or groups depending on how many computers are available for student use.

Directions

- Prior to beginning class, the teacher will review the appropriate use policy of the school for using computers with Internet access.
- Review the graphs studied in class for the past few weeks including bar and pie graphs.
- Have students walk around the room and interview their friends, asking one specific question (e.g., *What is your favorite subject in school?*)
- Ensure students document all results.

- After gathering their data, have students use the computer to create a bar and a pie graph and record their findings.
- After creating two charts, the teacher will review the data and ensure it is recorded correctly.
- Then have students activate the Jing software and record a video of both graphs on their computer screen. Be sure students address what each graph shows, the differences in the two charts visually, and which graph shows the data most effectively in their Jing video.
- If available, have students upload their video to the class blog.
- Allow time for students to view and comment on their peers' graphs.

References

Bender, W. N., & Waller, L. (2011). *The teaching revolution: RTI, technology, and differentiation transform teaching for the 21st century.* Thousand Oaks, CA: Corwin.

McCrea, B. (2012, January 18). Designing the 21st century K–12 classroom. *The Journal.* Retrieved from http://thejournal.com/articles/2012/01/18/designing-the-21st-century-k12-classroom.aspx

TechSmith. (2012). *A few ways you might use Jing.* Retrieved from http://www.techsmith.com/jing-uses.html

Tech Tool 9

Gaming, ARGs, and Virtual World Instruction

What Do I Need to Know?

Instructional gaming was, by 2013, coming into its own as a viable instructional method (Miller, 2011a; Sheehy, 2011; Takahashi, 2012). Of course, teachers have used various game formats, including both gameboard- and technology-based games, for decades. However, as the commercial video gaming market has reached new highs in sales that are well into the billions of dollars, educators have begun to use tech-based games to teach important content (Miller, 2011b, 2012). Most importantly, the early data suggest that gaming and/or simulation scenarios are highly effective instructional tools (International Society for Technology in Education [ISTE]), 2010; Maton, 2011).

With those cautions noted, it is a fact that tech-based games have been employed as enrichment activities for some time in education, with no apparent ill effects. Computer-based games, such as the *Age of Empires* or *Civilization*, have long taught students how civilizations come into existence and fight for valuable resources. The decades-old *Oregon Trail* did an admirable job teaching recent generations of Americans what the settlers of the western frontier faced as they traveled across the continent in the 1800s. Even games developed for entertainment value have been used in schools. One teacher has used a popular game called *Angry Birds* to teach physics principles, while others have used popular, commercially available games such as *SimCity* to teach how complex systems interact (Sheehy, 2011).

Joel Levin is a second-grade teacher that wanted his students to learn computer skills, and in order to motivate them, he used the game *Minecraft*

(Sheehy, 2011). With that age group, Levin had to eliminate some game content, since some of the monsters and other game elements would not have been appropriate in a second-grade class. However, Levin reported that his students responded very well to the game format as they learned computer skills, as well as online etiquette, Internet safety, and even conflict resolution in a gaming context (Sheehy, 2011).

> Teachers are using the game *Angry Birds* to teach physics principles, and the *SimCity* game to teach how complex systems interact.

Today, many games have been developed specifically for teaching educational content across the grade levels, and the great news is that some of these games are available free of charge. For example, *Pemdas Blaster* (teaching the order of mathematical operations) and *Algebra Meltdown* are designed to teach a wide range of mathematics skills, and these games are aligned with the Common Core State Standards in mathematics (see Mangahigh at www.mangahigh.com).

One website we recommend is www.edutopia.org for a discussion of games in learning, though many other gaming websites are available offering a wide variety of games. Also, for a better understanding on the use of games for learning, teachers might wish to view a brief video on games in the classroom that is available from Edutopia.org (http://www.edutopia.org/blog/games-for-learning-community-resources-andrew-miller).

> Many games have been developed specifically for teaching educational content across the grade levels, and the great news is that some of these games are available free of charge.

The games at this site are targeted for students ranging in age from seven to sixteen. The games all stipulate a goal for students to achieve by repeatedly practicing the core learning concept, and teachers can track the progress of their students using their own login and passwords.

Teachers report anecdotally that these games result in students playing their math games long after school is over, and sometimes well into the night (see the website www.mangahigh.com for several teacher reviews). Certainly any mathematics teacher should take advantage of this website to access some educational games that will motivate most students.

BrainWare Safari is a set of game scenarios that are intended to strengthen certain cognitive skills, including skills in the areas of attention, memory, visual and auditory processing, thinking, and sensory integration (http://www.mybrainware .com/how-it-works). This educational software program is currently being used by teachers and home-schooling parents alike (Shah, 2012). The game is a cloud-based program (i.e., user performance data is stored on computers of the publisher) and operates like a video game. Over twenty different games are included, and each offers many levels of play and focuses on multiple skills.

> Teachers report anecdotally that games such as these result in students playing their math games long after school is over, and sometimes well into the night.

These games are sequenced and intended to help the student develop automaticity in the targeted cognitive skills. The developers recommend that students access the games three to five times weekly, and spend thirty to sixty minutes on the game each time they play in order to improve those targeted cognitive skills.

Alternative Reality Gaming for the Classroom

The newest innovation in educational games involves creation of or actions within "alternative realities" or an alternative world. These are referred to as alternative reality games or ARGs (Maton, 2011). In ARGs, students select a character (an avatar), and that character serves as an action figure that represents them throughout the game. In some ARGs, online actions and real-world assignments to be completed by the students are actually mixed, thus combining instructional experiences in the alternative world with tasks or assignments in the real world. A number of ARGs have been developed recently for educational use (Maton, 2011), in various settings ranging from public education to the US military. In fact, both industry and the US armed services use ARGs for teaching everything from individual combat tactics in confined spaces (e.g., city terrain) to airborne fighter combat. While ARGs are still being explored, these may represent nothing less than a fundamental paradigm shift in the future of education.

In ARGs, students are playing a role, and in most cases, these games are hosted by an Internet site rather than merely developed as software on a CD as were many earlier games. This provides the advantage of anytime-anywhere learning since students can play from home as well as school. It also provides the option to mix actions in the alternative world with actions in the real world. Today, ARGs may be played using school computers, home computers, or even smartphones or tablets, such as the iPad or Kindle Fire. If a student can access the Internet, he or she can play the ARG. Students complete the ARG activities working either individually or in teams. In many ARGs, students receive clues for the activity and other instructions, as well as feedback, during the gaming activity itself. They then complete activities online or in the real world.

> ARGs involve the creation of an alternative reality in which characters play a role and learn academic content during the game.

There are various examples of educational games described in the literature. One classroom teacher, Kevin Ballestrini, developed an ARG that placed the students' avatars in ancient Rome in order to teach them Latin (Maton, 2011). The students in the game were required to work online while wandering the streets of Rome, interacting with others and directing their character in Latin. Thus, the students had to plan, act, create, and write like a Roman citizen. During the game the characters helped to rebuild the city of Pompeii. Students had to find inscriptions on stones and solve mysteries during that process, thus learning the language and applying it in ways not possible in a more standard Latin classroom. That particular ARG is now being used experimentally in thirty classrooms across the United States, and the latest version can even be played using Internet-capable cell phones!

The Smithsonian Museum recently developed an ARG called *Pheon* (www .pheon.org), which was launched in the fall of 2010. *Pheon* uses the traditional "capture-the-flag" type of game format, and teams of students compete to gather information on various online art exhibits. Further, for students who live near the museum itself, *Pheon* has a real-world component and thus, the game can be played in the real world at the museum itself. However, like many modern ARGs, this game involves more than merely acquiring information. One activity in the game requires students to take a digital picture of their favorite tree (or other living object) and post that to the *Pheon* website. In that way, students are actively contributing information to the museum.

In fact, with those photo contributions, students are creating information that will ultimately be placed within a massive online catalogue of biological species worldwide! That multinational project is called the *Encyclopedia of Life*, and is intended to create a digital archive of every species on Earth. Students find their studies highly engaging when they are actually contributing knowledge to the world in some format. By participating in this ARG, students are not learning exclusively in a passive, receptive fashion any longer. Rather, students are also actively crowd-sourcing or contributing to online content in a format that will be available worldwide. For most students, this type of activity is highly motivating.

A Sample ARG Lesson

Here's a sample ARG-based instructional lesson. A seventh-grade US history class is studying the antebellum period and the Underground Railroad. A simulation ARG has been developed to teach what that experience was actually like for enslaved persons trying to escape slavery. *Flight to Freedom* is a simulation game that was designed

> By participating in this ARG, students are not passive learners, but are actively creating information, and, in some cases, contributing to online content in a format that will be available worldwide

specifically for teaching that content and to illustrate the use of games in education. This simulation helps students experience the struggles of slaves in the antebellum South as they attempt to escape into freedom in Canada. We recommend that teachers who may not be experienced with educational games spend fifteen to twenty minutes going through part of that ARG by actually playing this game for a time (http://ssad.bowdoin.edu:9780/projects/flighttofreedom/intro .shtml).

Like most such games, *Flight to Freedom* can be played either individually or by small groups, and is intended for students from the midelementary grades through high school grades. In this game, the player (or players) are presented the opportunity to choose one of nine historic African American characters from that antebellum period as an avatar (e.g., Sojourner Truth, Frederick Douglas, Harriet Tubman). Players then read a brief biography of that character, and use that character within the game itself; all avatars are then placed on a map somewhere in the southern states.

Each avatar has a "status board" presented on the computer screen, that describes that character's circumstances, including overall health, financial resources, and a description of the situation in which the character finds himself (e.g., hiding in a barn in Alabama or crossing a wilderness creek in Tennessee). The student then has to make choices as to what his avatar must do to avoid getting caught while escaping to Canada. Options include trying to escape from the current situation, remaining in place, or seeking information about family members. The overall goal of the game is for each character and family to escape into Canada, and each decision a student makes holds consequences for the avatar in terms of costing money, damaging health, or being recaptured and taken back into slavery.

> Most educational games can be used as an adjunct to the class in order to help students actually experience their learning content firsthand.

Like most educational games, this game could be used as an adjunct to the class in order to help students experience the learning content firsthand; in this game, students will sense the overwhelming odds against escaping slaves. While lectures, texts, and videos could be used to teach this same content, students are much more likely to sense what those enslaved persons actually felt when they were confronted with the same types of choices during their escape to Canada. In short, this ARG makes the study of this content a much richer experience for the students, resulting in much higher levels of engagement, and ultimately, higher mastery of the subject material.

To sense the potential of this learning option, imagine the entire school curriculum, in the near future, in which all subject areas are taught via educational games and ARGs! While curricula in most areas have not developed to that point as of 2012, teachers should still explore gaming and ARGs that might be appropriate for their grade level and content in order to remain current with 21st century classroom instructional methods. ARGs for the classroom are quite likely to dominate future educational endeavors.

> Imagine a future curriculum in which all subject areas are taught via educational games and ARGs!

3D and Virtual World Instruction

A number of schools are experimenting with 3D and virtual worlds as instructional tools of the 21st century, and in some sense this represents a step beyond the ARGs described above. Unlike scripted games in ARGs in which the content to be mastered is set in advance, 3D instruction in a virtual world is unscripted. Thus, a teacher and the class can create virtually any world they wish as a basis for study of content related to that world ("Georgia District," 2012; "Scientists Caution," 2012). In that sense, the teacher or the class is effectively creating an ARG, but the content is whatever the teacher and class decide upon.

There are various examples of 3D virtual worlds being used as instructional tools today. For example, sixth-grade students at Nature Hill Intermediate School in Wisconsin recently studied history and English in a virtual world called *Quest Atlantis* ("Game-Based Learning,"2012). In that multiuser 3D game-space, students direct avatars in various missions, while interacting via chat functions with other avatars, on the content under study. Also, the material written by students must be evaluated and accepted by the "Council" (who is, in reality, the teacher), so virtually all written material can be checked and evaluated. Coupled with a BYOD (bring your own device) initiative at the school, students are involved in gaming technology in many different areas.

Teachers should be aware that some of the virtual world locations are completely unregulated, and thus, some degree of caution is in order. For example, in the virtual world site, *Second Life* (secondlife.com) is the largest three-dimensional virtual world on the Internet. Here, all users can socialize, connect with each other, and create content or "worlds" that focus on any topic whatsoever. Many educational institutions, including for example, Harvard University and Ohio State, are creating worlds to all students world wide to audit college level classes. There are a number of worlds in which students can experience actually living in historic locations (e.g., Pirate Island). Teachers might preview a specific location that teaches about history or science and then have students access that location only in class when the teacher can directly supervise their learning.

However, students using that site are completely unprotected, and various locations within *Second Life* are specifically developed for meeting or virtual-world sexual interactions that are clearly not appropriate for students. Further, almost every avatar on that site is actually a real person, interacting simultaneously with everyone else at the same *Second Life* location. Thus, various avatars on that site can be literally anyone on Earth, including a number of persons that teachers would not want interacting with students in the public school classroom. For these reasons, we do not generally recommend *Second Life* for use in the public schools; but some teachers are using it, and we wanted to present it here to illustrate the caution teachers must use in selection of virtual world sites. More protected sites are recommended.

As one example of a more protected option for virtual world instruction, schools in Forsythe County, Georgia, have the option of using the *OpenSim* platform (http://opensimulator.org/wiki/Main_Page), and this open-source software allows educators to create virtual worlds related to their class content ("Georgia District," 2012). That system will allow district administrators to deliver virtual world learning to engage students in authentic problem solving and promote student creativity within the virtual world. Role playing is used, as in all ARGs and virtual worlds, and students act out their lesson content in science, social studies, mathematics, or other content areas. As one example, the developers have built a model of the Berlin Wall in order to teach students about the Cold War period in history ("Georgia District," 2012).

Virtual world or 3D instruction is quite likely to be a definitive element of instruction in the 21st century, and we felt it necessary to present this as an instructional option that some educators are using today. However, this instructional approach is new and schools are only now beginning to explore this virtual-world instructional option. Further, creation of virtual worlds for instructional purposes involves a set of skills that many teachers do not posses presently. For this reason, we do not recommend that teachers who are not quite familiar with educational gaming launch themselves into use of virtual worlds in the classroom. Rather, we do urge all teachers to experiment a bit with the use of educational games in their subject area, and ARGs that may fit nicely within their content. Once teachers have determined how to best use those instructional options, they might consider creation of virtual worlds as a basis of instruction.

Advantages of Games, ARGs, and Virtual Worlds

There are several advantages to teaching with games, ARGs, and virtual worlds that have been mentioned previously. Perhaps the most important single advantage is that today's C2S2 students are highly motivated to complete schoolwork when the content is presented in game formats (ISTE, 2010; Miller, 2011a, 2011b). In fact, for many C2S2 kids, gaming is a preferred after-school activity as well as an in-class expectation. For this reason, the early data on gaming or virtual worlds in the classroom, though mostly anecdotal, does suggest that games and educational simulations are effective instructional tools (ISTE, 2010; Maton, 2011; "Scientists Caution," 2012). Games and simulations can teach content in important, exciting ways, and these tech tools have the advantage of actually putting the student into the situation or event under study. This advantage alone has already motivated many educators to explore game- and simulation-based instruction.

Educational games and role play in virtual worlds tend to increase academic achievement for many students today (Ash, 2011; Maton, 2011). Because games seem to work as an instructional technique, many curricula being developed today include games to accompany online texts, and curricula developed for stand-alone learning, such as the Khan Academy, employ game formats to motivate C2S2 students to complete their studies (see Tech Tool 5). Further, many teachers have anecdotally reported that their students enjoyed learning in technology-based gaming formats (Ash, 2011; Maton, 2011), and that they saw benefits from these games in terms of students' achievement overall.

> The early data, though mostly anecdotal, suggest that games and educational simulations are effective instructional tools.

Next, many educational games, ARGs, and virtual world activities are interactive, and interaction can greatly enrich the learning experience. In fact, interactive games allow many students to play the game and thus master the content at the same time and offer either individual or team play. Further, depending on the game, that type of competition can involve students in different locations worldwide. Imagine the impact of having American students, Canadian students, students from London and students in France compete in a simulation game focused on the Seven Years War. While that war in the Western Hemisphere was called the French and Indian War, it was in fact a much more global conflict, in which France and England were fighting, as were all of their colonies. Interaction such as this, including the option of worldwide interaction, can be quite motivating for students, and while such options can be difficult to arrange, instructional gaming provides the promise of such exciting options in the near future.

Another advantage of modern games is the richness of the video content. As almost any parent realizes, kids love video games, and the video presentations become more real with each passing month. Most modern games come complete with highly complex video presentations, and such visualization options can boost learning, as the examples above illustrate. Further, the complexity of this video content makes these games seem similar to activities that many students today choose to do via their home gaming consoles. Gaming is quite enjoyable for many students and that seems to be the main reason that games increase student engagement with the content, which in turn, increases achievement ("Scientists Caution," 2012; Sheehy, 2011).

However the debate on the effects of gaming is still on-going ("Scientists Caution," 2012; Shah, 2012), and there may be negative effects of gaming. In fact, in several oriental cultures, where games have become much more entrenched,

> The debate on the effects of gaming is still on-going, and there may be negative effects of gaming.

some have even suggested that gaming might be addictive to young minds (Dretzen, 2010). Of course, that concern is focused on commercial games that are played strictly for personal enjoyment, rather than educational gaming, and to date that issue has not become a major concern relative to educational games used in the classroom.

How Do I Begin Using Gaming, ARGs, and Virtual World Instruction?

Step 1: Carefully Select Several Games or Virtual World Websites

Many websites offer educational games for content at various grade levels; some are free and others require a nominal monthly fee. The websites below will provide you with some gaming resources for your class, and for more selections, we suggest that you do a Google or Bing search for indicators such as "educational games middle school science" or "games elementary health."

www.funbrain.com

www.knowledgeadventure.com

www.playkidsgames.com

www.edutopia.org

primarygames.com

pbskids.org

www.sheppardsoftware.com

funschool.kaboose.com

www.arcademics.com

opensimulator.org

Step 2: Match Games or Virtual Worlds to Your Content!

Of course, finding educational games is merely the beginning. Teachers should carefully select games that match the content under study, as well as the Common Core State Standards and any state standards that may apply. While gaming is a great activity that students are supposed to enjoy, teachers must select games to maximize student learning, and some games have much richer content than others. Also, teachers must consider their use of the game. Is the game to be used for initial instruction or practice of previously learned content? Different uses can inform which games or ARGs teachers might use in the classroom.

While we presented several examples above of teachers creating educational games, we generally do not recommend that unless a teacher is highly fluent with technology. Further, we do not recommend that most teachers attempt to "import" content into games, as that can be quite complex, and teachers typically need highly developed technology skills to do so. Rather, we recommend that teachers attempt to draw the natural lessons from the game content itself (Sheehy, 2011), and then relate those to the Common Core or state standards that might apply in a given instructional unit.

> We generally do not recommend that teachers create games or ARGs unless they are highly fluent with technology.

Step 3: Preview the Game

Of course, teachers must preview any game or ARG selected for classroom use; in many cases teachers simply play the game they have selected one time. This preview will allow the teacher to determine possible uses of the game and, in many cases, set up different levels of the game for students at various academic levels. While a preview is essential initially, once a teacher begins to know and trust the games available at a given website, he or she might be able to merely implement those games and activities without a preview or use other resources from that same location with increased confidence.

Step 4: Beware of Fee-Based Games or Sites

While there is nothing inherently wrong in fee-based games, we do recommend caution with fee-based sites, since costs can quickly mount. Fee-based sites for games that involve a set monthly access fee, or a per-student fee that is set for the year, are the best locations for teachers to use, as those costs can be predicted in advance. In some cases, school administrators will find some funds to cover these costs, but many teachers likewise have found games so useful that they occasionally pay these fees themselves.

Step 5: Relate Game Themes to Nongame Content

Games, ARGs, and virtual worlds in the classroom are most effective as educational tools when the relationship between game activities and the content under study in the instructional unit is highlighted. While some games present these relationships well, others do not, and it is ultimately the teacher's role to demonstrate for the students the relationship between the game and the content under study. Thus, for many games, some type of post-game activity that reinforces the instructional content is appropriate, particularly if games are used during the initial instruction phase of the instructional unit.

Step 6: Teach Cyber Safety!

> It is ultimately the teacher's role to demonstrate for the students the relationship between the game and the content under study.

As the caution above indicates, instructional games, and in particular real-time ARGs, provide teachers an opportunity to teach about cyber safety and appropriate use of the Internet. While we discussed this issue in the introduction for this book, we mention this again here, because interactive gaming is likely to become a large segment of education in the future, but student safety should always be paramount. The guidelines presented in the introduction can certainly apply here, and teachers should repeatedly advise their students never to provide any personal information in that context, unless that is directly supervised by the teacher.

How Do I Differentiate Using Gaming, ARGs, and Virtual World Instruction?

Educational games, ARGs, and virtual worlds offer many options for differentiating instruction. First, in instructional gaming, students are required to act more independently than in traditional classroom activities, and they are also much more active in the learning process. Given the student selection options built into most educational games, students tend to differentiate themselves within these gaming scenarios by their selections and choices within the game, particularly in ARGs that mix online and real-world activities. Linguistically talented students, for example, are likely to select game activities that focus on language-based learning options, whereas students with a visual learning strength will select more visual activities.

Next, in setting up the parameters of the game or ARG, teachers can create many differentiation options for their students. Depending on the game, many factors can be preset by teachers such as the activities within the game, the level of play selected for and by various students, or the pace of the activities. In making those choices with individual students in mind, teachers can differentiate the content and the process within the game. Thus, differentiating the instruction during instructional gaming is not difficult, and students are almost always highly motivated to participate in these types of highly differentiated learning activities.

> In gaming environments, students are forced to act more independently than in a traditional classroom environment, and thus, they are typically much more active in the learning process.

Conclusions

It is hard to imagine tech-tool options that hold more promise for education than educational gaming, ARGs, and virtual world instruction. These instructional options are increasingly being applied in industry and other endeavors such as the armed services. The senior author of this text experienced an excellent instructional simulation in the course of learning to become a private pilot! However, the potential of ARGs and games is only beginning to be recognized by the educational community (Ash, 2011; "Georgia District," 2012; Maton, 2011; Miller, 2011b, 2012), and teachers have to search to find a content-rich gaming experience for the classroom. Still, we recommend that all teachers explore this tech tool, as implementation of tech-based educational games, ARGs, and simulations certainly represents the future of education.

References

Ash, K. (2011). Games and simulations help children access science. *Education Week, 30*(27), 12.

Dretzen, R. (Director), & Rushkoff, D. (Writer). (2010, February 8). Digital Nation [Television series episode]. In R. Dretzen (Producer), *Frontline*. Boston, MA: WGBH/Public Broadcasting Service (PBS). Available at www.pbs.org/wgbh/pages/frontline

Game-based learning catching on in schools. (2012). *eSchool News*. Retrieved from http://www .eschoolnews.com/2012/05/08/game-based-learning-catching-on-in-schools/

Georgia district implements virtual world technology. (2012). *eSchool News*. Retrieved from http:// www.eschoolnews.com/2012/03/28/Georgia-district-implements-virtual-world-technology/

International Society for Technology in Education (ISTE). (2010). *How can technology influence student academic knowledge?* Retrieved from http://caret.iste.org/index.cfm?fuseaction=evid ence&answerID=12&words=Attention

Maton, N. (2011). *Can an online game crack the code to language learning?* Retrieved from http:// mindshift.kqed.org/2011/11/can-an-online-game-crack-the-code-to-language-learning/

Miller, A. (2011a). *Game-based learning units for the everyday teacher.* Retrieved from http:// www.edutopia.org/blog/video-game-model-unit-andrew-miller

Miller, A. (2011b). *Get your game on: How to build curricula units using the video game model.* Retrieved from http://www.edutopia.org/blog/gamification-game-based-learning-unit-andrew -miller

Miller, A. (2012). *A new community and resources for games for learning.* Retrieved from http:// www.edutopia.org/blog/games-for-learning-community-resource-andrew-miller

Scientists caution that more research is needed to prove benefits of video games in education. (2012). *eSchoolNews*. Retrieved from http://www.eschoolnews.com/2012/01/l1/researchers -debate-gamings-effects-on-the-brain/

Shah, N. (2012). Special educators borrow from brain studies. *Education Week, 31* (17), 10.

Sheehy, K. (2011). *High school teachers make gaming academic.* Retrieved from http://education. usnews.rankingandreviews.com/education/highschools/articles/2011/11/01/high-school -teachers-make-gaming-academic?PageNr=1

Takahashi, P. (2012). Schools seeing improvement in math scores as students play video game. *Las Vegas Sun*. Retrieved from http://www.lasvegassun.com/news/2012/feb/08/school-district -seeing-improvement-math-scores-stu/

Tech Tool 10

Diigo

What Do I Need to Know?

There is no question that students today are inundated with information from the Internet and social media. This massive amount of available information is what prompted The Partnership for 21st Century Learning Skills to advocate that each 21st century learner achieve informational literacy or the ability to manage information from a variety of sources, use it accurately, and evaluate it critically (Bender & Waller, 2011; "Framework for 21st Century Learning," 2004). This is a lofty order for our students considering the amount of time they spend on the Internet and the variety of sources (accurate and inaccurate) available. How can we, as teachers, ensure that our students not only collect appropriate information when they do research but also learn the difference between a valid and invalid source; that they learn to evaluate everything they are reading with a critical eye?

Diigo: A Social Bookmarking Tool

This is where an online bookmarking tool such as *Diigo* can truly serve our students. Diigo is a social bookmarking tool that allows teachers to capture content on a single topic, including titles of articles, videos, or other digital information, and make that available for students. Using Diigo, we can build a set of articles, videos, or other informational items, and scaffold our student's exposure to information on a given topic. This tech tool helps teachers organize information and scaffold articles and other sources to teach our students how to deal with the abundance of information available (Bender & Waller, 2011).

121

Definition: Diigo is a social bookmarking tool that allows teachers to capture content on a single topic, including titles of articles, videos, or other digital information, and make that available for students.

Diigo is a cloud-based tool that supports online and collaborative research with the integration of sticky notes, highlights, tags, and screen capture functions. When using Diigo, teachers and students bookmark (or save) websites into their libraries, which can then be made public. Then either teachers or students can use the Diigotools to make notes and annotations associated with those bookmarked articles to assist with further research. Teachers and students using Diigo can gather articles and information into coherent folders and then use the social networking features built within this tool to share their findings with others. Thus, Diigo in the classroom promotes collaborative learning as students are able to manage the information they encounter online during research together. To learn more about Diigo, teachers may wish to view an overview video at http://www.vimeo.com/12687333. Once there, just click and check out "What is new in Diigo V5.0."

Here is an example of how Diigo might be used in the classroom to promote informational literacy and critical thinking skills. A teacher using Diigo might set up a reading list combined with ongoing assignments, or the teacher might save articles about particular current events for her students and use the highlight feature within Diigo to accentuate important sections of the articles (McCrea, 2012). Using the sticky-note feature, the teacher can then ask students questions about the article, have them delineate fact and opinion statements as well as leave their own questions posted directly onto the article. Once the students have analyzed the teacher's article, they might then be required to search the Internet for their own article about that same current event. Once they find an article, the students should be expected to use the Diigo features to include their own notes and compare and contrast the information and the accuracy of information found by their peers. All of those articles, and the relevant notes, would then be collected within the Diigo class library for review during and after the unit.

> Diigo is a cloud-based, social bookmarking tool that supports online and collaborative research with the integration of sticky notes, highlights, tags, and screen capture functions.

Diigo also promotes collaborative research among groups of students and under the educator accounts; student groups have all of the features of regular groups on Diigo. Teachers can apply for an educator account, and once approved, student accounts can be created for all members of the class (with or without using student e-mails). Once a class is created, the students are automatically entered in as a Diigo group, which means that students can share articles, Internet links, and bookmarks with peers; annotations are seen by the group and group forums can be visited.

Because this is cloud-based, a teacher can assign a research topic for one group of students and create a subgroup on Diigo for this research team. The students can then research articles from their home or school computer, add links to the team's group account, highlight and make notes about information that should used, and discuss together the usefulness of each article. Instead of having to spend the entire class period in the library working in groups to finish the assignment, students can work interactively during and after the school day as long as they have Internet access.

This collaborative nature also benefits teachers who teach more than one section of a class. For example, a science teacher who teaches AP Biology twice a day may encourage the students in either class to collaborate in order to foster further peer input. Thus, Diigo facilitates cross-class collaboration in research as students share annotations, sticky notes, and comments—a form of collaboration that would normally be impossible.

> Because this is cloud-based, a teacher can assign a research topic for one group of students and create a subgroup on Diigo for this research team.

Teachers in any subject area can introduce new content material and have students complete an Internet search to preview the upcoming material. They may find articles and then highlight particular sections with questions that the teacher can address during the unit of study. This is one way for teachers to activate the students' prior knowledge while at the same time using their input and questions to drive instruction.

We strongly recommend utilizing the educator's account on Diigo for privacy reasons. When using the educator's account, any ad presented is education-related, and the default privacy settings assure that only teachers and students can communicate within the account. Further, with those default privacy settings in place, student accounts are not made available through any public searches.

Professional Development with Diigo

Teachers can also join various professional development groups on Diigo and use various teaching ideas to differentiate material for students in virtually all subject areas. Under the "My Groups" tab in Diigo, for example, you should click on "Search for a group" and enter the type of professional development group you wish to join. Groups are available on anything from "Technology in the classroom" to "Simple differentiation ideas in math."

Becoming a member of these groups and searching through articles found within each group will guide you in other ways to differentiate material for various student learning styles and levels. As teachers, we must remember that we set the example for being lifelong learners and we must find ways for our students to see us continuing to grow in our education. We, as educators, know that students need a 21st century education (Rivero, 2012), and now we need to find the best possible ways to ensure all students are mastering the 21st century literacy skill as well as the content skills that they need. Joining other educators through social bookmarking will help you stay current and relevant in your teaching and your own personal growth. To begin, you may wish to check out the Diigo website (http://groups.diigo.com/browse?cg_id=21) for a complete list of educator groups available on Diigo, and here, these groups are categorized into subjects and themes.

Selecting a Social Bookmarking Tool

There are several things to consider prior to using any social bookmarking site in the classroom. First, Diigo is merely one social bookmarking tool available to teachers, and because it has been around for a while, more educators use this tool than any other bookmarking site. Diigo has gained widespread popularity among teachers for collaborative research and professional development, and we do recommend this site for those reasons. However, there are other bookmarking options available. Two of the more popular alternative bookmarking websites are *Delicious* and *Pinterest*.

Delicious (www.delicious.com), is a social-bookmarking website that is very similar to Diigo, and many teachers use that site also. It may be the largest bookmarking site worldwide with over 5.3 million users, but it is generally more focused on publically shared information than on private bookmarks and information, though privacy settings are available. This is free to use for anyone worldwide.

Pinterest (www.pinterest.com) is a relatively new, free social-bookmarking website that has only recently been described in the literature (TEEContributor, 2012). Nevertheless, teachers are signing up for this bookmarking site in droves. This site is structured like a pin board, on which teachers can pin photos that represent the content, rather than merely a link (as in Diigo), and some believe this makes Pinterest a better site for educators than Diigo (TEEContributor, 2012). In that sense, Pinterest becomes a visual organizing tool. Some teachers look for lesson plan ideas on Pinterest, while others share their Pinterest board with colleagues who may be teaching the same subject. In order to share content with students, it may be advisable to set up a new Pinterest board for each curricular unit (TEEContributor, 2012). Anyone over thirteen years of age can establish a Pinterest board, but all Pinterest users must be invited to participate, which is one way the Pinterest site assures safety for its members.

When choosing which site to consider for your bookmarking needs, teachers may wish to consider the number of users a given website hosts, the documentation available to help you differentiate between articles (tags, lists, etc.), and the amount of help available through the service provider. Finally, teachers may choose to use one bookmarking site (perhaps Diigo or Delicious) for classroom use, and another (e.g., Pinterest) as their site to share professional development ideas or teaching resources with their colleagues. At the very least, teachers should check out the several options available and choose the server that best fits their needs.

How Do I Get Started Using Diigo?

Step 1: Create an Account

To begin using Diigo, visit www.diigo.com/education. You will need to create a free standard Diigo account as a first step. Once you have signed up for the standard account, you will need to apply for the educator's account which will include giving your school e-mail and answering a few questions about how you plan to use Diigo with your students.

Step 2: Install the Toolbar

Once you have signed up for the appropriate Diigo account, you will need to install the Diigo toolbar. You will find the link to do that under the "Tools" heading at the top of the page. Diigo provides explicit direction for how to install the toolbar on your personal computer.

Step 3: Create Groups

To create your class group, go to the "My Groups" tab and click "Create a group." You will need to name your class group and also scan through the various settings available.We recommend making your page a private page so that only members of the group (i.e., your students and perhaps a school administrator) can view the content. We also suggest that you limit the search results so that searches do not show up in public pages. You should also make your group an "Invitation only" group, and ensure that only you, as the group moderator, can invite new members. Once you have selected these privacy settings, you will be able to create a safe, secure group for your students.

Step 4: Add Student Accounts

Student accounts will be added through your Diigo teacher dashboard. When these accounts are created, students will be limited to communication with their classmates and teachers. There are many other steps that can be taken to make groups into class groups and to join in with other teachers to create one large group. For explicit steps to take when creating student groups, visit http://help.diigo.com/teacher-account/faq.

Step 5: Bookmark One or More Articles

Once you have uploaded the Diigo toolbar, researching and bookmarking takes a few simple steps. When either you or your students find an interesting webpage and wish to bookmark it, open the Diigo toolbar and click "Bookmark." You will then be given the option to create tags for your article which will make it easier to search for your article later. If you are using the article for a particular class, you might write the class name as a tag or select the content of the article as another tag option. Anything that will help students find the article later can be used. Also you might wish to add in a description of the article so someone searching through the library is able to easily identify the content.

If students are using these items in their research, you might have them add in detailed descriptions that include summaries of the various articles, their critique of each, and perhaps an explanation as to why some articles were good sources. Having students practice these skills over time will promote informational literacy that they will need for a lifetime.

Step 6: Create Content-Specific Lists

You can also create lists in your library to organize bookmarked articles. Creating lists for the class helps organize any articles found. You should create lists for particular content material being studied, specific research topics, and perhaps for collaborative learning groups within the class.

Step 7: Use Other Diigo Features

Teachers and students alike will also have options for interactive discussion on each webpage. By clicking on the Diigo toolbar, students and teachers can highlight various sections of the article and leave sticky notes for others to see and respond to. All of these actions take place from the Diigo toolbar.

How Do I Differentiate Using Diigo?

Diigo provides opportunities for teachers to store varying resources for differing student groups, and in that sense, teachers can differentiate their lessons somewhat. For example, a seventh-grade science teacher introducing the study of the atmosphere may create two or three different Diigo lists in the class group library for her students. One list might have resources that are on a higher grade level for her students needing enrichment, another list for her on-grade-level students, and finally another list with resources for those students functioning below grade level. Although all of the content would feature the atmospheric study, the reading level of the articles in each list would vary depending on student need. Continuing with the same example, the teacher can also differentiate the lesson at a higher level. With the class divided into groups, the teacher can differentiate further by addressing each group separately with the sticky note and highlight features available in Diigo. For her higher level group, the teacher may post sticky notes on each article with application questions or other higher-order thinking tasks that encourage the students to dig deeper into the content material. She may also have those students search for additional relevant articles on the topic. In the list of resources for lower-functioning students, the teacher may have each student highlight and post their own questions so that she can see where she needs to spend more time in instruction.

However, homogeneous groups within the class represent only one instructional option using Diigo. Should the teacher wish to form heterogeneous groups within the class, Diigo can be an excellent tool to use in a

> Diigo can be an excellent tool to use in a jigsaw-type of cooperative-learning assignment.

jigsaw-type of cooperative-learning assignment. Different groups might have access to different sources and different highlighted notes on each source, and in that context, students across the groups would need to pool their knowledge in order to gain a complete understanding of the topic. Incorporating tech tools such as Diigo into tried-and-true instructional activities, such as jigsaw activities, will enhance the interest levels of the students and enrich the activity overall.

Finally, Diigo can help a teacher scaffold information for the class. While factual links and articles should be initially delivered via Diigo early in an instructional unit, later in the unit, more complex ideas in different articles might be made available to the class as a whole or to specific groups within the larger class. Such scaffolding is a key to building deep understanding of concepts, and Diigo can assist in that regard. As these examples illustrate, either Diigo or these other social bookmarking sites can facilitate differentiated instruction in a variety of ways.

A Sample Lesson Plan Using Diigo

Standard: Common Core State Standards—Reading Standards for Literacy in History/Social Studies
>   **Grades 6–8: Standard RH.6–8.1 Key Ideas and Details**
>   Cite specific textual evidence to support analysis of primary and secondary sources.
>   **Grades 6–8: Standard RH.6–8.6 Craft and Structure**
>   Analyze the author's purpose in providing an explanation, using specific language, describing a procedure, or discussing an experiment in text.

Students will . . .

- Read and analyze several articles selected by the teacher
- Find their own text aligning with the content material
- Post critical thinking questions for their peers to answer
- Choose one peer article and answer the questions posted there

Materials

- Access to a computer with Internet capabilities
- A Diigo student account for each student

Preparation

- Set up student accounts in Diigo for each student in the class
- Create a group for your class
- Create a list delineating the topic of study
- Bookmark two or three articles related to topic of study
- Highlight various sections in the articles and post interactive sticky notes discussing author's purpose and textual evidence that supports analysis of secondary source

Directions

- Introduce the content material being studied and have students log in to Diigo and open up the articles you have bookmarked.
- Walk through the articles and discuss the author's purpose in the article. Identify specific language that illustrates the author's purpose, and have students highlight particular sections of the article that support their analysis of the author's purpose.
- Complete this same activity with another article on the same content material.
- After discussing the articles posted by the teacher, ask each student to find one article relating the content under study (review the acceptable use policy together, discussing appropriate and inappropriate searches on the Internet).
- Have students bookmark their article in the list section for the class.
- After finding the article, have students post questions throughout the article about the author's purpose using the sticky note and highlight features available in Diigo.
- Have each student choose one article posted by a peer and go analyze the article with the questions from their peers. Have them answer the questions directly on the sticky notes posted.

Conclusions

Social bookmarking is a teaching tool that we recommend for all teachers. In fact, this tool can strengthen instruction in a variety of ways. Allowing students to utilize the interactive features of Diigo incorporates the 4 C's the Partnership for 21st Century Skills advocates for every child—creativity, communication, collaboration, and critical thinking (Rivero, 2012). Student creativity is sparked as they search for their own articles on content matter instead of sitting back and having information handed to them. Their ability to communicate with peers and teachers via the Diigo features helps students practice formulating their own opinion in a concise manner; collaboration is promoted as students in various groups work together to find pertinent information; and their critical thinking skills are challenged each time they search for a relevant article.

Once a teacher has mastered the first four tools in this text, he will be in a position to explore many other tech tools, and certainly Diigo or other social-bookmarking sites should be high on that list.

References

Bender, W., & Waller, L. (2011). *The teaching revolution: RTI, technology, and differentiation transform teaching for the 21st century.* Thousand Oaks, CA: Corwin.

Framework for 21st century learning. (2004). *Partnership for 21st Century Learning Skills.* Retrieved from http://www.p21.org/index.php?option=com_content&task=view&id=254&Itemid=120

McCrea, B. (2012). 5 K-12 e-learning trends. *THE Journal.* Retrieved from http://thejournal.com/articles/2012/02/02/5-k12-e-learning-trends.aspx

Rivero, V. (2012, February 14). Partnering up for 21st-century skills. *EdTech Digest.* Retrieved from http://edtechdigest.wordpress.com/2012/02/14/interviewp21timmagner/

TEEContributor. (2012). *Pinterest! An amazing resource for teachers.* Retrieved from http://h30411.www3.hp.com/posts/1421030-Pinterest_An_amazing_resource_for_teachers?mcid-Twitter

Part III
Tech Tools for Student Creation and Collaboration

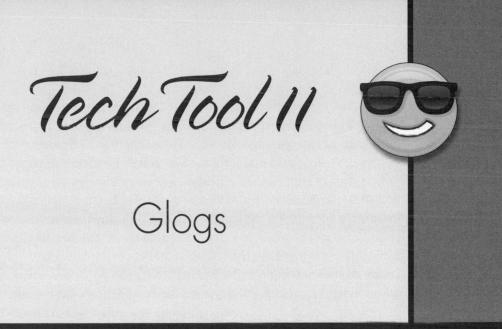

Tech Tool 11

Glogs

What Do I Need to Know?

One critically important aspect of tech-tool teaching involves providing the option for C2S2 students to create information, and while student creation has traditionally been emphasized in education, in the 21st century classroom students' creation of information is considered critical. In a traditional classroom, students were invited to create information in many forms including position papers, themes, proofs, and book reports. As that list indicates, each of those creation options is completely dependent on the tools then available in the classroom, that is, paper and pencil. Today any or all of those assignments can be implemented using 21st century creation and information-sharing tools, and using these modern tools has two important effects: (1) students become much more motivated to participate in assignments when they are invited to create information, and (2) students become much more proficient at the types of brainstorming and information creation tasks that are common in the 21st century work environment.

The next tools presented provide a variety of exciting options for student creation of content. In that sense, these tools represent the evolution of the teaching-learning process, from a process that in the past viewed students as passive receivers of knowledge, to a future in which students are creating new knowledge and solving real-world problems. Not only will social learning characterize the teaching-learning process in the future, but student creation of content provides exciting opportunities to move into 21st century instruction today using these tech tools.

A *Glog* is the first example of such a "student creation" tech tool. Simply put, a Glog is a multimedia file, poster, or presentation that is created digitally and that can be developed and used by either the students or the teacher. Creating a Glog allows students to creatively display their understanding of course content. *Glogster* (edu.glogster.com) is the online web service that provides a platform for Glogs. Using Glogster, students log in to a safe web space to create their digital multimedia files, which can be developed either individually or as a team project. This resource can be used across all the public school grade levels, and children as young as four years old, working individually or as a group, have used this site to create Glogs.

> **Definition:** A Glog is a multimedia file, poster, or presentation that is created digitally, and that can be developed and used by either the students or the teacher.

The website uses templates which make the entire process easy for students with various levels of technology experience. With simple point-and-click actions, students can hyperlink pages from outside websites, videos from YouTube or TeacherTube, or images from the Internet. This provides the student with the ability to hyperlink outside websites and videos, and forces students to learn important research skills while also checking the validity of sources. Glogs can also support data attachments, photos, videos, graphics, sounds, and drawings.

> The user-driven process of creating a personal Glog engages the student completely, allowing each student to spend more time with classroom content while also building digital literacy skills.

When using Glogster, students can work independently or in small groups to create a multimedia book report, showcase information on mathematics problem solving, or present particular science or social studies content. Schools around the country are using web applications such as Glogster to create interactive classrooms online. Students work together in the virtual classroom to create, study, peer edit, and present ("Open High School," 2011).

As described by the *New York Times Teaching and Learning Blog* (Ojalvo & Schulten, 2010), the user-driven process of creating a personal Glog engages the student completely, allowing each student to spend more time with classroom content while also building digital literacy skills. In this sense, students today are creating content rather than merely studying content, and that is one way that the basic teaching and learning process is being transformed by modern instructional technologies (Bender & Waller, 2011).

While Glogs are being created, teachers can monitor student work through the teacher dashboard, depending on the level of subscription services used (see section "How Do I Get Started With Glogster?" below). Once a Glog is finished, the student can publish it so that peers can view his work and comment on the virtual poster. Although Glogs can be published as "Public for all," teachers have the option to keep any Glog private for their individual classroom. Any comments posted on the Glogs can also be monitored by the teacher. These features enable the teacher to create a safe virtual classroom. While student safety is a fundamental concern, we generally recommend schoolwide publication via a school website or the "Public for all" publication only after a Glog has been completed and evaluated by the teacher. Such publication increases student participation and allows students to show their work to their parents, both of which should always be encouraged.

There are many other uses for the completed Glog. For example, if an interactive whiteboard is available in the classroom, teachers can display the Glog so that students can also practice oral presentation skills. Glogs can also be embedded on class blogs, wikis, or webpages, allowing for continual review throughout the school year. In a sense, embedding the content-rich Glogs creates an ongoing textbook for each classroom. Using the Glogster service creates a digital learning environment that is easily scalable for each student. Students are able to share their content knowledge in innovative ways and in a secure virtual classroom.

How Do I Get Started With Glogster?

When starting with Glogster, teachers have the option to use the free Glogster service or upgrade to various Glogster premium accounts. A

Single Free Teacher account is an individual account where a student or teacher can create and save private Glogs only. To use this free service, each student would need an individual e-mail address and would need to register. To view any work, the student has to give the teacher the URL address of the complete Glog.

To have access to student accounts, teachers must purchase at least one of the three membership packages starting at $30 a year. Each level of membership offers various advantages including Glogs without advertisement, tech support, document-attachment features, extra graphics, class messaging, and even more direct access to student accounts. The "Teacher Light" Membership will allow teachers to manage student accounts from a teacher "dashboard," and students do not need personal e-mails to register. We recommend that teachers begin by using the free version and then decide if this platform of expression works for you and your students. If so, you can always upgrade the services once you find you are using it frequently.

> Teachers have the option to use the free Glogster service or upgrade to various Glogster premium accounts.

Once a membership level is decided upon, students can log in and begin to create their personal virtual poster. Specific instructions for doing so are presented below, and that section of this book may be printed and distributed to students for an easy tutorial. Also, there is a great deal of information on the Glogster website (edu.glogster.com), and we recommend that teachers spend some time familiarizing themselves with the various options there prior to using this resource.

How Do I Differentiate Using Glogs?

Teachers using Glogster have multiple options for differentiation within the context of creating virtual posters. Glogs provide an opportunity for content differentiation in the process and product of learning a particular unit. As one example, when students are studying the water cycle, a teacher might have those students needing an extra challenge seek out and view various videos online to document the stages of the water cycle. Those students can then create a Glog with required videos in their Glogs. The students would be required to upload the video, organize the Glog content, and write some text summarizing the main points. Those Glogs can then serve as supporting study content for the more challenged students. Further, students needing extra help during the unit on water cycles would also be required to incorporate videos, but the teacher can select particular videos for them that present the stages of the water cycle more clearly.

Thus, in order to differentiate this instructional content, all students would be given the opportunity to create a Glog but the level of depth incorporated would change based on students' needs, learning styles, and abilities. Those students who might feel intimidated by writing an entire essay on the water cycle may find comfort in the short text requirements associated with developing a Glog. As the student becomes more comfortable with the content, students can use their Glog information to create a more in-depth research presentation or theme paper.

> In order to differentiate this instructional content, all students would be given the opportunity to create a Glog, but the level of depth incorporated would change based on students' needs, learning styles, and abilities.

Teachers can also consider student learning styles when assigning Glog creation. Visual learners may opt to incorporate more video on their Glog while other students may select more text or animation. Allowing students to utilize those components that are most effective for their learning styles enhances content engagement and increases student motivation to participate actively with the content under study.

Finally, teachers can also differentiate by deciding if students need to work individually, in tutoring pairs, or in small groups. Students needing extra help in the content area can work alongside a partner to share ideas but also have guidance in content choices and descriptions. In many cases, having students work together increased the engaged time for most students with learning difficulties, and a peer buddy is likely to keep them more task-oriented.

Examples and Other Useful Resources

A Sample Lesson Plan Using Glogs

The following lesson plan is based on educational standards from North Carolina, and it involves the culmination of a unit studied in a fifth-grade science classroom in that state. Competency Goal 3 in the North Carolina Standard Course of Study (NCSCOS) requires that students "conduct investigations and use appropriate technology to build an understanding of weather and climate."

As one assessment component for that instructional unit, students worked in small groups to create Glogs showing content mastery. To enhance student motivation and to allow for differentiation, students were able to choose from the following unit projects.

Project 1: Final Product

NCSCOS 3.01: Investigate the water cycle and the processes of evaporation, condensation, precipitation, and run-off.
Students will create an in-depth Glog presenting each phase of the water cycle. The Glog must depict why each phase of the water cycle is imperative.

Process:

1. Research each phase of the water cycle carefully and record the most important information found during research.
2. Find one video or animation on the Internet that depicts each phase of the water cycle.
3. Create accompanying text for each phase describing why that phase is an invaluable part of the cycle.

Project 2: Final Product

NCSCOS 3.05: Compile and use weather data to establish a climate record and reveal any trends.
Students will take an in-depth look at precipitation and the precipitation in our community and our Skype Pals' community. Students will create a Glog depicting the similarities and differences between their community weather patterns and our patterns.

1. Students will research the precipitation patterns in our community for the past six months.
2. Students will research the weather patterns in our Skype Pals' community for the last six months.
3. Students will then create a Glog with a graph attached showing each weather pattern. The graph should be accompanied by a short text describing the similarities and differences.
4. Pictures should be included from each community displaying the weather.
5. A summary text should be incorporated on the blog describing how the weather patterns affect the way we live in our community and the way our Skype Pals live in theirs.

Project 3: Final Product

NCSCOS 3.03: Describe and analyze the formation of various types of clouds and discuss their relation to weather systems.

Students will research the various types of cloud formations and be ready to explain their impact on the weather systems. Students will then choose one weather system that frequents our community and discuss what would happen if that type of system did not occur again.

1. Students will record the various types of cloud formations and their impact on the weather system.
2. The Glog should have a picture or video of each cloud formation and its subsequent weather system with accompanying text summarizing the picture.
3. Students should choose one weather system discussed and show how the absence of that weather system would affect our community. Pictures and animation need to be utilized for the viewer to truly understand the impact.

Step-by-Step Guidelines for Creating A Glog

These are step-by-step instructions for teacher and student use in creating a Glog. This should be done after a teacher has become somewhat familiar with the Glogster website.

Begin by going to www.edu.glogster.com.

1. Click on "Log in."
2. Enter your username and password that the teacher gives you!
3. Click on "Create a New Glog."

4. Let's create a blank screen for you . . .

- Click on each picture part and then click on the red trashcan—that makes it go away!

5. To make a background click on "Wall." Choose the one you like. Click "Use it."

- Then you have to close the box with the x.

6. To add words click on "Text." Choose the box you like. Click "Use it."

- Then you have to close the box with the x.
- Click on the box and then click "Edit."
- You can start typing. When you are done click "OK."

7. To add pictures click on "Graphics." Choose the picture you like. Click "Use it."

- Then you have to close the box with the x.

8. To add a picture from the Internet, you need to open a new window and find the picture you want to use.

- Then click on the picture and save it.
- Then go back to Glogster and hit "Image."
- You'll then hit "Upload."
- "Find and select" the picture you had.
- Then click "Use It."

9. To add a video from the Internet, you need to open a new window and find the video you want to use.

- Then click on the website address and copy it.
- Go back to Glogster, hit "Video."
- Then, click on "Link."
- Then paste your video in.
- Or you can search through the SchoolTube videos and find one you like.

10. When you are done, don't forget to save it!

- Give it a name.
- Click on the bubble that says "School."
- Click "Unfinished" if you are not done.
- And then "Save."

Conclusions

For decades teachers have used posters in the classroom, and the most effective use of such images has always been the teacher's frequent use of the poster content, while pointing out how the poster presents various topics, or images, in relationship to other images. In the 21st century classroom, it seems only natural that this instructional tactic will be transformed into digitally created posters, and we do encourage teachers to explore the use of Glogs in the classroom, either as teacher-developed teaching tools or as student assignments.

References

Bender, W. N., & Waller, L. (2011). *The teaching revolution: RTI, technology, and differentiation transform teaching for the 21st century.* Thousand Oaks, CA: Corwin.

Ojalvo, H., & Schulten, K. (2010, July 9). Tech tips for teachers: Free, easy, and useful creation tools. *The Learning Network: Teaching and Learning with the* New York Times. Retrieved from http://learning.blogs.nytimes.com/2010/07/09/tech-tips-for-teachers-free-easy-and-useful-creation-tools/?nl=learning&emc=al

Open high school of Utah makes learning "collaborative, interactive, and flexible." (2011, June 7). *eSchool News.* Retrieved from http://www.eschoolnews.com/2011/06/07/eschool-of-the-month-open-high-school-of-utah/

Tech Tool 12

Podcasts

What Do I Need to Know?

What teacher hasn't faced the challenge of creating review sheets and handouts prior to exam week or end of grade testing? In fact, going back from June to the beginning of the year in order to extrapolate the most important content material can overwhelm even the master teacher. Further, once the information is gathered, getting students excited about reviewing this material can be quite a challenging task. This is where the use of a tech tool such as *podcasts* throughout the year can truly benefit a classroom teacher.

A podcast is a video or audio multimedia clip about a single topic typically in the format of a radio talk show. Podcasts are accessed online and can be downloaded from the Internet onto your computer or, in the case of audio podcasts, onto an MP3 player. What differentiates a podcast from any other video or audio clip available on the Internet is that users can subscribe to a particular podcast so that their computer will automatically download the latest episode when available. Using a service called RSS (Really Simple Syndication), a podcast works in a way similar to a magazine; users subscribe and the latest one appears on their computer. Podcasts can also be found through services such as iTunes. Podcasts have two basic functions: to retrieve information and to disseminate information (Eash, 2006), and both of these can be quite useful for teachers and students.

> **Definition:** A podcast is a video or audio multimedia clip about a single topic typically in the format of a radio talk show.

142

There are podcasts available on virtually any subject imaginable, so they can easily be found and utilized to rouse student interest in new content material (Bender & Waller, 2011). Many podcasts that can be used in the classroom may be found on Apple iTunes, as well as on various tools that can assist teachers in using podcasts. Here are some examples. A sixth-grade teacher in social studies might wish to discuss different economic systems in South America and Europe, and a podcast on that topic could be used to compare those systems. Searching for and playing a podcast straight from the selected area in Europe or South America would give students real perspective on the situation and help them make connections between what they are reading in class and what is actually happening around the world. Although some podcasts require paid subscriptions, the majority are available for free download (check the Extra Resources section at the end of this section for a list of free educational podcasts).

As mentioned previously, teachers can use Web 2.0 tools and create their own podcasts on new content material. With minimal tools, teachers can create podcasts that are shortened versions of class lectures on the latest content material. These podcasts can then be uploaded to class wikis or blogs which would serve various purposes—review for students who need extra help and information for students who may be homebound or absent. Keeping a catalog of podcast minilectures also provides a library of review material at the end of the semester or school year. In one sense, each of the 2,700 videos available in Khan Academy (see Tech Tool 6) might be considered a podcast on a specific type of problem. Also, podcasts provide the basis for the flipped classroom concept as discussed previously.

Alternatively, students may be required to create podcasts on topics under study, making this an excellent option for fostering student creativity. Of course, teachers would review and critique such podcast content prior to using that podcast as a tool for teaching the content to other students. However, students do enjoy creating content, and this will engage students in ways that more traditional studies cannot. Students will enjoy listening to podcasts from the Internet or their teacher but being able to participate in the creation process will certainly increase their motivation (Bender & Waller, 2011; Eash, 2006). Having to research, write, edit, and publish the podcast script quadruples the amount of time students are spending with the content material, helping them internalize, apply, and understand the information. When students are required to create their own podcast, they also have to learn how to research, write, speak fluently, manage their allotted podcast time, and secure a listener's attention. All of these skills are vital for our 21st century learners. Once students have created their own podcast, their voice is suddenly connected to the world in a new and exciting way (Eash, 2006).

Here is an example. Imagine a fifth-grade teacher teaching about the ecosystem. That teacher might break students up into three groups and have

> Students will enjoy listening to podcasts from the Internet or their teacher but being able to participate in the creation process will certainly increase their motivation.

each group research one part of the system (producers, consumers, and decomposers). Groups would be responsible for creating a five-minute podcast detailing the functions of their organisms within the population of the ecosystem. Students would need to research the information, write their podcast script, edit the script, and finally publish the podcast. Once students have completed their section, they would upload the audio file to the class blog and then in turn listen to their peers' presentations as well. By mastering the content of each of the podcasts, the students will have a complete understanding of ecosystem parts and functions. Further, that content would remain available for those students as a study guide, for the remainder of the school year.

Going back to our original dilemma involving the end-of-year review, a teacher who has throughout the year created and uploaded podcasts to a class wiki or blog already has a library of review material in the form of podcasts for each student. The podcasts are now available, both at school and at home, for each student with Internet access, and these short podcasts will help students review the most important material that was covered throughout the year.

How Do I Get Started Using Podcasts?

Step 1: Finding Podcasts for the Classroom

There are several ways to find podcasts related to your classroom content. The easiest way to find specific material is simply to conduct a Google search for content you need. If you are searching for information on the Pythagorean Theorem, you would type in the search engine "podcasts on the Pythagorean Theorem," or if you wanted poetry podcasts, you would create the same type of search. This will give you a list of various websites that provide podcasts related to your specific material. For a quick add-on to your lesson, pull the podcast up on your computer and play it through your interactive whiteboard so that students can hear the content.

Step 2: Review the Podcast First

Generally, we recommend that teachers review the podcast initially to assure that the content is appropriate and presented at the desired instructional level. Of course, it is quite appropriate to use podcasts that present information at varied levels, as one differentiated instructional option in the class.

Step 3: Set Up an RSS Feed

If you find a specific podcast series that discusses relevant information for your students each week and you would like to continually utilize the information, you may wish to set up an RSS feed for that podcast series. Setting up such a feed allows you to subscribe to the podcast series, and you will be constantly updated with the new podcast episodes. For most podcast series, it is relatively easy to set up such a feed. First, locate the podcast's webpage and find the "Subscribe" button. You will probably need to choose the way you would like to receive notification of a new episode. If you have iTunes on your computer, you can choose that option, and the new episodes will be automatically uploaded to your iTunes account each week. If you do not use iTunes, you choose the option for Google and the RSS feed will show up on your Google homepage and alert you that a new episode is available. From that Google page, you can click right on the link and go directly to your latest episode.

Step 4: Upload Podcasts for the Class

Once you have an RSS feed on your Google page, you will need to make those available for your students. To make these episodes available to students, you will need to upload the podcast files onto your class wiki or your class blog so that students can consistently access each episode. Any episode you would like to share on your blog or wiki first needs to be saved onto your hard drive. Just right click on the episode link and follow the "Save as" directions including finding a location on your hard drive and naming the file.

Once you have saved the podcast onto your hard drive, you will need to create an account with an online site that will provide you with the appropriate links for uploading podcasts. One such service is www.divshare.com. Creating an account is free at *Divshare*, making it an ideal selection for educators. To create an account you only need to supply the website with your e-mail and password.

Once you have created an account, find the section that reads "Upload new file." A search box will appear and you will need to find the episode name on your hard drive. Once you have located the appropriate podcast, simply click the upload button and Divshare will take care of the rest. When the upload is finished, you will see a link at the top of the page for your document. Once you click on the link, you can choose to "Embed" your podcast. If you click on the embed option, you will be given an extraordinarily long code to copy. Copy that code and move to your blog or wiki. On your blog or wiki you will need to switch to "HTML view," paste the link, and then switch back to the normal or "Visual view." When you switch your views, you will see the podcast appear as a small radio or audio player and your students can simply click play to listen to the episode. The podcast is now available for any student wishing to access the information and will be archived for the remainder of the school year.

Step 5: Create Your Own Podcasts

Finding and sharing podcasts that have already been created is one way to motivate and engage students. However, allowing students to create their own podcast takes their involvement with content material to a much higher level (Eash, 2006). The tools you will need to create a podcast are minimal—a computer with Internet access and a microphone. To create your podcast, download editing software such as Audacity (http://audacity .sourceforge.net/). Once you have downloaded the program onto your computer, you will see a screen for podcast creation. Simply click on the red "Record" button and start your episode. When you are finished, click the "Stop" square. You can replay your podcast to ensure accuracy by simply clicking the "Play" button. There are many other options for editing available on Audacity that may be of interest to you or your students for a more professional-sounding podcast.

Step 6: Publish the Podcast

Once you are satisfied with your episode, go to "File" and click "Export." This will give you the opportunity to save your podcast on your hard drive. Then you will need to name your podcast and determine where you would like to save it. We recommend using a name that delineates the exact content on the podcast, since that name will help you and students in later years search for specific content. Once you have done that, you can follow the steps outlined above to upload the podcasts onto wikis or blogs for everyone to view.

How Do I Differentiate With Podcasts?

Options for differentiation are endless once a teacher learns to podcast. A national survey by MetLife on college and career readiness reveals that teachers in the United States feel that differentiation is essential for student success, and they claim that access to technology makes differentiation possible ("Stakeholders Differ," 2011). Teachers feel that greater access to a variety of instructional tools would greatly improve their ability to teach diverse learners ("Stakeholders Differ," 2011), and the creation of podcasts in the classroom involves using cheaper, Web 2.0 technology tools to reach every student. Teachers have the ability to use podcasts to challenge those students who need extra enrichment and at the same time podcasts can be used to provide intervention for students who are struggling with content material. Podcasts can be intentionally selected or created to present information in a variety of ways, or even in ways other than those typically used by a particular teacher. Podcasts can be found online that take the content material to a higher level, and teachers can provide links to these podcasts for their higher-level students. These students can see how the content material is being utilized in everyday scenarios and discuss the implications of this content material with their peers. At the same time, teachers can look for podcasts that explain the material in more detail or on a lower grade level for those students who need that intervention option.

Students who are excelling in content material may also be tasked with creating their own podcast. Teachers can have them synthesize the information in a peer-tutoring format and upload the podcasts for other students in the classroom. Students may also be asked to take the content a bit further and create a podcast depicting real-life application of the material or discussing the implications of the content in society today.

> Podcasts can be intentionally selected or created to present information in a variety of ways or even in ways other than those typically used by a particular teacher.

Once a teacher notices a small group of students struggling in particular content, a podcast can be created so that they can review the material at home. The podcast may offer a variety of ways to solve a problem or more practical examples, or simply recap the lesson. Students are able to access the podcast at home and are instantly connected to the material outside of the school day. Students would also be able to utilize the peer-created podcasts to gain further instruction, and, as all veteran teachers realize, students will sometimes pay more attention to a class peer explaining a concept than to the teacher explaining the same concept. Being able to access these podcasts at home encourages students to study further in problem areas in a nonthreatening environment.

Podcast creation assignments can also be varied in order to assure students success on a given task. Students who are more inclined to write may produce the script for a podcast, while other students may be more excited about the actual speaking part. Kinesthetic learners may be excited about the set-up and filming or recording of the podcast. Putting learners in appropriate groups ensures that each learner is able to work on a task that highlights individual talents while each learner is still intricately connected to the content material.

Teachers have often reflected on what technology might mean in their teaching. For example, teachers working with students from low-income families state that access to online and other technology-based resources would greatly impact their ability to differentiate material for each student ("Stakeholders Differ," 2011). Podcasts offer the chance to differentiate for a fraction of the cost of other online programs. If teachers have even one computer with Internet access in their class, they can find and download free podcasts on virtually every subject imaginable. Further, if teachers can find a computer with Internet access and a microphone, their students can participate in the creation of their own podcast. Thus, podcasts are one of the least expensive Web 2.0 tools that teachers can use, and these represent an excellent way to foster student creativity.

 # *Other Useful Resources*

A Sample Lesson Plan for a Podcast

Standard: Common Core State Standards—Reading: Foundational Skills, Grade 4: RF.4.4. Read with sufficient accuracy and fluency to support comprehension—read on level prose and poetry orally with accuracy, appropriate rate, and expression on successive readings.

Students will . . .

- Select a reader's theater script that is appropriate for a podcast
- Rewrite the script if necessary to fit the number of students in each group

- Read their assigned section fluently
- Record a podcast of the chosen script
- Discuss the overall theme of the script using expanded vocabulary and background knowledge

Materials

- Computer with Internet access and microphone for each group
- Access to http://www.teachingheart.net/readerstheater.htm for reader's theater scripts

Preparation

- Ensure that each computer has the Audacity recording program
- Create groups that include diverse learners with a variety of learning strengths (writers, readers, actors, producers)
- Prerecord several short podcasts with examples of good and bad fluency so students understand the overall goal of the assignment
- Create a short dialogue for students to practice in pairs (three to five sentences for each student in the pair to recite)

Directions

- Prior to beginning class, review the acceptable use policy with students.
- Discuss fluency with students and how fluency is important for understand text content and meaning.
- Play the prerecorded podcasts and have students evaluate the fluency in each one.
- Have students get into partner pairs and pass out practice dialogues. Allow several minutes for practice and then have partner pairs come forward and recite for the class. Let students offer constructive criticism on fluency rate.
- Divide students into groups and have them look on the website http://www.teachingheart.net/readerstheater.htm for a reader's theater script they would like to perform.
- After students have had adequate time to rehearse their script, allow them to use the Audacity program to record their podcast.
- When students have completed their podcast, upload it to the class blog and allow them to present the podcast to the entire class.

Sources for Free Podcasts to Enhance Instruction

http://www.teachingheart.net/readerstheater.htm

This is a great podcast that enables students to hear audio recordings of poems. Use it during poetry month as inspiration for a writer's workshop or to find a poem related to a thematic unit of study (Richards, 2012).

http://www.scientificamerican.com/podcast

This podcast offers a daily episode of science news. Students will learn anything from why we shouldn't use portable electronics in airplanes to why a black hole may eat asteroids. Each episode is packed with science information in just sixty seconds (Richards, 2012).

http://www.bookwink.com

Subscribe to the Bookwink podcast for three-minute videos and podcasts that feature different books. Watching these will get students excited about the new book they will read. If the RSS feed isn't sending you the book you want to read about that day, check out the website and browse by genre or grade level (Richards, 2012).

http://inklesstales.wordpress.com

Inkless Tales has stories, poems, and songs in podcasts for kids. Students can hear classic stories and poems such as *The Princess and the Pea* and stories rewritten by the authors themselves. Play these podcasts in your listening centers and have students answer comprehension questions or use as part of your writer's workshop.

http://grammar.quickanddirtytips.com

This podcast has weekly podcasts for older students that discuss confusing grammar rules. Use this as a creative way for students to critique their writing or use it in your ESL classroom.

Conclusions

How many times have adults noted that most students seem to be permanently glued to their iPod? Again, using student-preferred activities as a teaching tactic is likely to increase student participation, at least initially, with the lesson content. Also, podcasts are available currently on many topics, and having students search for appropriate podcast content in a lesson, perhaps as a component of the webquest assignment, can generate a variety of effective podcasts that teachers can then use in subsequent lessons. Further, the C2S2 students today do seem to enjoy receiving content in this form, though listening to music is certainly different than hearing a podcast on the distinction between the New Deal and the quantitative easing economic policies of today. We do encourage teachers to explore the use of podcasts and use their students in the searching process.

References

Bender, W., & Waller, L. (2011). *The teaching revolution: RTI, technology, and differentiation transform teaching for the 21st century.* Thousand Oaks, CA: Corwin.

Eash, E. K. (2006, April). Podcasting 101 for K-12 librarians. *Computers in Libraries, 26*(4). Retrieved from http://www.infotoday.com/cilmag/apr06/Eash.shtml

Richards, E. (2012). *10 Podcasts for teachers and kids.* Retrieved from http://www.scholastic.com/teachers/article/10-podcasts-teachers-and-kids

Stakeholders differ on college and career readiness. (2011, March 8). *eSchool News.* Retrieved from http://www.eschoolnews.com/2011/03/23/survey-teachers-want-more-access-to-technology-collaboration/?ast=77&astc=7085

Tech Tool 13

Scribd

What Do I Need to Know?

We cannot overstress the importance of providing today's C2S2 students with the opportunities to collaborate on their work, and ultimately share their work, with a larger audience. While many of the tech tools mentioned so far in the book are used to promote student collaboration and creation, perhaps one of the most basic essentials for creation and sharing is that of written documents, and it is clear that the ability to create and publish work is highly motivational for C2S2 students (TEEContributor, 2011). Such collaborative work also takes into account their desire for social learning and interconnectivity, and as noted previously, students' use of social media sites, such as Facebook and Twitter, show that students want to share their thoughts and work with their peers and social community. To disregard the simple fact that students love to publish (TEEContributor, 2011) is to miss out on an opportunity to motivate our students when it comes to interacting with content material.

Scribd and Web 2.0 Publishing

While students are creating many types of media in the 21st century classroom, perhaps the most basic type of communication is still a document of some type, and to facilitate collaborative creation and publications of documents, we recommend using *Scribd*. Scribd (pronounced "Scribbed") at www .scribd.com is the largest of the Web 2.0 publishing websites for social reading, and it allows teachers or students to post written work for all students to read. Currently, the site includes over 60 million users. It has been around for some time now, and over the last five years, many educators have explored the use of this tech tool. In essence, Scribd allows teachers and students to upload and transform any file—including PDF, Word, and PowerPoint—into an online document that's discoverable through search engines. Thus, the students' creation can be shared on social networks worldwide and read by billions of readers.

> **Definition:** Scribd is the largest of the Web 2.0 publishing websites for social reading, and it allows teachers or students to post written work for all students to read.

From the perspective of teachers, Scribd essentially serves two purposes in the classroom: teachers can both upload and download documents, and teachers or students can publish their own work worldwide. These functions allow teachers and students to share documents with the broader Scribd community. Uploading documents onto Scribd allows users to share their work with the Scribd community and the possibilities for uploads are practically endless for teachers. For example, teachers may wish to upload class notes for students who miss class, or PowerPoint presentations developed by either students or teachers. Teachers can also upload and share lesson plans with other team members in their schools or any other teachers worldwide interested in that same content. Scribd is able to house more than simple word documents, and teachers can upload books and puzzles, brochures, catalogs, illustrations, and maps. School administrators can upload school handbooks for community stakeholders and pertinent forms for parents including movie policies, Internet usage contracts, and field trip forms.

Scribd also allows users to download information from the growing community of readers. This lends itself to professional development for teachers. Others have shared their lesson plans, classroom management ideas, and discipline contracts on Scribd and you can simply search and download for your own use. Scribd does encourage those who are downloading to share their own documents in order to be a contributing part of the community.

There are books that are published on Scribd that can be accessed and read through the site. Some books are published in their entirety, whereas other users publish excerpts of books. As an example of how Scribd is used by fiction authors, the senior author of this text (using the pen name Jimmy C. Waters) has recently published the first chapter of his newest historical fiction novel on Scribd—*Taking Atlanta: Civil War in Georgia* (http://www.scribd.com/doc/89856384/Taking-Atlanta-Civil-War-in-Georgia). From the perspective of an author, this publishing site can get some early comments on one's work or provide some information on how many persons might be interested in a document with that title. These excerpts generally provide enough content for a user to become familiar with the general content of the overall theme of the book, and many education books are initially presented on Scribd. Teachers can use these excerpts to select class texts or to have students choose which books they would like to use for reports and research.

Student uses of Scribd are virtually unlimited. Students can use the download feature to access any documents posted by their teacher or school administration. Further, with a Web 2.0 publishing tool like Scribd, the development of student reports, themes, and other documents can become highly collaborative. Students can jointly develop and edit their documents or download the research of their peers. Like Diigo, Scribd provides an opportunity for students to practice their critical thinking skills and informational literacy as they sort through available documents for validity and accuracy ("Framework for 21st Century Learning," 2004). For a discussion of various uses of Scribd in the classroom, teachers should check out http://www.scribd.com/doc/28875411/Using-SCRIBD-in-Classroom.

Other Web 2.0 Publishing Options

We should mention that there are a number of similar Web 2.0 publishing options. For example, you may wish to consider Flipsnack (www.flipsnack.com). With Flipsnack, you can upload your PDF files and turn them into virtual flipping books on the computer—allowing students to see their stories in a book format instantly. Tikatok (www.tikatok.com) is an online publishing site where younger students can add graphics and text to a story starter or to a blank page and then turn their story into a virtual book or order a hard copy. You might also check out Issuu (www.issuu.com) which allows for the uploading of any document format and then transforms the document into a flipping book. The final product created can be embedded into class blogs and wikis (TEEContributor, 2011).

How Do I Get Started with Scribd?

Step 1: Creating an Account with Scribd

If you have a Facebook account already, Scribd will allow you to log in and begin the upload/download process immediately with your Facebook account. This also gives you the option to "Share" and "Like" various documents and have those show up on your Facebook profile for your friends.

If you do not have a Facebook account, you can still create a Scribd account. You will need to provide Scribd with your e-mail address and then create a username and password. From there you can begin posting and downloading.

Step 2: Uploading Your Documents

When you login to Scribd, you will see the official Scribd toolbar at the top of the screen. There will be a place for you to search out documents you wish to download as well as a blue "Upload" button. To upload your document, simply click "Upload" and follow the steps provided by Scribd. Scribd lets you choose between uploading from your computer and importing from Google Docs (see Tech Tool 15—Google Apps for more on Google Docs).

When uploading from your computer, simply find the document you wish to share and highlight it. Once you do that, you will have to agree to the Scribd terms and policies including copyright laws. You also have the option at this point to make the document private if you do not wish to share it with the Scribd community.

Once you have completed the upload process, be sure to give your document plenty of descriptors by adding in tags, descriptions, categories, and titles. The more information you provide about your document, the easier it is for users to find it. To build a larger following on the Scribd community, follow other publishers and readers (teachers, educators, administrators, etc.). The more that you upload and comment on other's documents, the more followers and readers you will have on your own account.

You can access the documents you have uploaded at any time by clicking on your account name at the top right-hand side of the toolbar. When you click on your name, use the drop-down arrows to find the tab reading "My Documents." This will take you to any document you have uploaded onto your account. From there, you can edit the document, upload a revision document, delete it, change it from private to public, or share it via Twitter and Facebook.

Step 3: Downloading Documents

Downloading documents from the Scribd library is a fairly easy process. Simply use the search box as you would any search engine to find the topics you are interested in. Once you find a document that interests you, there are several options for downloading and sharing. You can download or print the actual document, embed the document onto a wiki or blog, or "Readcast" the document (which means share it on your Facebook or Twitter account).

If you have uploaded documents for your students, have them "Follow" you on Scribd so that they will see any new documents you upload. Once they have an account and are following you, they can simply click on your account name and picture to see any documents you have uploaded for the class. You can also provide them with the exact name of the document you uploaded so that they can search for it via the search bar. From there, students will be able to download the documents they need to access.

Step 4: Creating Collections

Scribd allows you to group your documents together in "collections" so that they are easy to find based on content or theme. This will help you organize the various documents you upload and download on your account. You can create a collection for lesson plans that you research from other teachers, lesson notes for your students, documents for parents, and a collection of articles for students to read. This will make it easy to navigate your findings and easy for your followers to find the document they need.

To create a collection, start again under your Scribd username at the top right-hand of your toolbar and click on "My Collections." From there, you will simply need to click on the button "Create a New Collection," name the collection, and then decide if it will be public or private. Private collections can only be seen by the user whereas "moderated public" collections can be edited by any user. We suggest creating "locked public" collections where students and others can access your collection but cannot make changes or add documents.

When you have a document you wish to add to a collection, go to your "My Documents" page and find the document. From there you will see an option for adding the document to a collection and you can choose the collection that the document belongs in.

Step 5: Considering Security Issues

We would like to caution that, at this point in time, Scribd does not have an educator's account with heightened security. Scribd is considered a public domain and student work will be available for all Scribd community users. There is an option for making documents private, but students and families should be made aware of the public nature of the site. We also recommend that all students and their families be required to sign a permission slip allowing the use of such sites.

How Do I Differentiate With Scribd?

Differentiating instruction with Scribd is similar to using Diigo in the classroom where resources can be selected and stored for particular student groups depending on need. Teachers can assign varying text to small student groups based on reading and instructional level, and even provide differing levels of study guides for specific Scribd documents.

Teachers using guided reading groups can utilize the book excerpts available on Scribd for group time. Guided reading is an instructional strategy that provides explicit systematic instruction to a small group of students and has been shown to be an effective literacy intervention (Bender & Waller, 2011). Scribd provides an entirely new library of authentic literature to choose from when trying to work on various phonological skills with students in these guided reading groups.

Since Scribd supports various types of file formats, differentiation can also be based on student learning styles and interests. Students needing visual representation of content material may find the comic uploads more useful, while those students needing a mathematical representation of the content may find the puzzle uploads helpful. Teachers can upload various representations of the content from brochure form for concise summaries of material to visual maps so that students are able to access the material that helps them understand in the most effective way possible.

Like Diigo, Scribd can be used to scaffold student information in content material as well. After presenting basic instructional material, teachers can upload more in-depth application articles for students to utilize. This type of learning builds upon itself, providing an opportunity for students to slowly build a deep understanding of content material.

Scribd in the Classroom

Scribd can be used in a fashion similar to Diigo in the classroom, and we would suggest that teachers refer to the previous section on Diigo (see Tech Tool 10) to see a sample lesson plan. Below are some other suggestions for use of Scribd in the classroom.

- Upload your lesson plans and share them with other teachers in the Scribd community.
- Search for and download lessons for your own classroom from other teachers.
- Upload class lecture notes for students who missed class or are homebound. You can leave them as a document on Scribd or embed them from Scribd onto your class blog or wiki. If you have a class Facebook page, you can also share the document there.

- The ability to leave comments on Scribd documents provides an opportunity for interactive discussion. Have students upload their papers and let their peers leave constructive criticism for peer review.
- Keep a portfolio of writings to show growth throughout the year for each student. These writings would be accessible anywhere there is Internet access instead of hidden away in a teacher's desk drawer.
- Post important school documents including handbooks, permission slips, calendars, and policies for student and parent access.
- Upload student PowerPoint presentations and papers for parents to see. This helps establish and strengthen the home-school connection.

Conclusions

Scribd is one of the most commonly used publishing sites, and it allows teachers and students to publish their work to a worldwide audience. Having students' work available in this format can foster increased student participation and even help tie in parents to the activities in the classroom. While sharing of videos, images, and animated content is important for C2S2 students, there is no more basic need than the sharing of written documents, so we encourage teachers to explore the application of this tech tool in their classrooms.

References

Bender, W., & Waller, L. (2011). *RTI and differentiated reading in the K-8 classroom.* Bloomington, IN: Solution Tree Press.

Framework for 21st century learning. (2004). *Partnership for 21st Century Learning Skills.* Retrieved from http://www.p21.org/index.php?option=com_content&task=view&id=254&Itemid=120

TEEContributor. (2011). *9 Web 2.0 sites to publish work.* Retrieved from http://h30411.www3.hp.com/posts/13034389_web_2_0_sites_to_publish_student_work?mcid=Twitter

Tech Tool 14

Comic Life

What Do I Need to Know?

The tech tools discussed previously facilitated student creation and collaboration in a variety of formats including digital posters (Tech Tool 11—Glogs), development of audio/video podcasts (Tech Tool 12—Podcasts), and collaborative creation of written documents (Tech Tool 13—Scribd). Still, the Web 2.0 options for student collaboration and creativity do not end there! Why not use comic strips as well, a form of written work that students overwhelmingly enjoy? In fact, given the popularity of comics in C2S2 students today, this only seems a natural for teachers.

Comic strips have been popular with students for many decades, and more recently, graphic novels have captured students' imaginations. Graphic novels are generally between fifty and one hundred fifty pages, and include short novels that are presented in both script and comic or cartoon pictures. Because of the incredible and enduring popularity of this communication and book format, the power of using a comic strip as an educational tool should not be underestimated. Introducing written comics into the classroom increases engagement with the content under study, improves writing skills, and focuses many students on the content at hand (Stillwell, 2011). Comics can be used to help students in both reading and writing. For example, comics can serve as a bridge to help students practice complex reading skills before transferring those reading skills to larger texts or literature assignments ("Using Comics," 2005). Allowing students to use comics in the classroom provides them with an opportunity to visualize what they are reading, and thus, this format for reading instruction will help many reluctant and struggling readers succeed ("Using Comics," 2005). Following the format of a comic also helps students understand plot line. In this format, students are able to see the basic story elements and follow the story, or even create their own work ("Using Comics," 2005).

Comic Life is a user-friendly software program available to help teachers and students create their own comic strips using the class content (http://comiclife.com). Any content that the class is studying can be the subject used for the comic strips, and allowing students to plan their story and then customize the characters and background provides an opportunity for authentic literacy. Students become intricately involved in every step of the creation process from planning to writing to creating (Lyga, 2006). Comic Life is compatible with Windows, Mac, and iPad software and hardware, making this usable in almost any classroom.

> Because of the incredible and enduring popularity of this communication and book format, the power of using a comic strip as an educational tool should not be underestimated.

Definition: Comic Life is a user-friendly software program available to help teachers and students create their own comic strips using the class content.

Students are given many options for creating a comic with Comic Life. They can drag and drop pictures from digital cameras, computer web cameras, scanned photos, or any other on-screen images into their comic strip and then add dialogue to create their story. They then add text boxes, thought balloons, speech boxes, or annotations to hold the written content, and they can even use various filters to customize their uploaded pictures, thus making those digital images appear to be hand drawn. Allowing students to work through the visual components of the creation process is likely to help them practice visualizing stories, and in turn, this visualization will help strengthen reading comprehension (Lyga, 2006).

The options for integrating Comic Life software into the classroom are virtually endless and teachers can find a plethora of these ideas at http://www.comiclife.com/education. Here are several examples from various academic areas.

- *History teachers* can have students create a comic strip detailing a timeline of events for a specific historical period.
- *Geography teachers* may require students to use geography content for a timeline on "Mountain Creation and Erosion!" Teachers may also

have students act as a "travel guide" and lead a walk through a given location under study.

- **Science teachers** might have students plan and create a comic strip to explain the experimental process they followed in a recent lab class and discuss what would have happened if a particular step had been left out.
- **English teachers** can have students write an original story in comic book form, or take on the role of a character they read about in class and explain in the comic strip, the character's thoughts, feelings, and actions.
- **Math teachers** can have students write comics to explain particular steps to solve problems and then discuss why each step is important to the process.

As these examples indicate, the applications of this tech tool are extensive and limited only by the imagination of the teacher and the students. Like most Web 2.0 tools, this tech tool will result in increased participation in the class, and students enjoy the creative aspects of learning in this format. Both individual participation and participation during group collaborative creation of comic strips is likely to increase.

How Do I Get Started With Comic Life?

Step 1: Consider Purchasing Options

To purchase Comic Life, visit the website and check out the various pricing packages available. If you are purchasing the licenses for your individual classroom, it will probably cost around $20 per license. You might consider purchasing only one or two licenses for your classroom and then letting students "rotate through" the use of the software.

Step 2: Practice With Comic Life

Once you have downloaded the software, you should spend some time learning the features prior to introducing this to your students. Teachers may wish to develop a comic strip themselves for use in class, prior to having students use Comic Life. It is always a good idea to put in digital photos of local scenes that students may recognize when creating a comic strip for teaching purposes.

Step 3: Choose a Template for the Assignment

There are a few basic steps involved when creating a comic strip with Comic Life. The first task is to choose a template and background for your page. There are over 2,000 templates to choose from and even a category devoted to education where you can find templates for comic strips about science projects, timelines, and historical events.

Step 4: Identify and Upload Photos

In planning a comic strip, teachers in lower grades may wish to provide the essential content themselves. Of course, older students may be required, as part of the assignment, to identify digital pictures for the comic strip, and many such pictures can be obtained from the Internet. Older students can easily upload photos from the hard drive of the computer or any other digital source. Depending on the age of the students, some teachers might wish to include a brief lesson on using copyrighted material as one component of this lesson. Once the photos are identified and uploaded, students can move to the next step of actually planning the comic strip.

Step 5: Storyboard the Comic Strip

A storyboard serves the same purpose in developing a video or comic strip that an outline serves in writing a theme. Depending on the age of the students, teachers may either plan the storyboard or outline for the comic strip for the students or have the students develop that outline. The storyboard can be planned based on a minimum of two elements: (1) the overall message or story theme to be included, and (2) an array of digital photos or drawings that can be used to communicate that theme. Older students, once again, can be provided a theme and work on collecting digital photos or drawings themselves, whereas teachers may need to provide these elements for younger students. Once the pictures are uploaded, all that is required is a simple drag and drop to place them into the appropriate locations on the comic strip, as suggested in the storyboard.

Step 6: Enter Text Content

Finally, an avenue must be chosen for entering text whether that is a thought balloon or lettering. Because the storyboard may include only a general theme for the comic strip, more text will need to be developed to communicate the content. Students may write text individually, or as a group for the various drawings or digital photos, and once the text is prepared, it should be placed next to the appropriate image. In Comic Life, students can stretch and modify the text containers to fit appropriately within their comic strip. This freedom for customization gives students a sense of independence and promotes creativity within each assignment.

Step 7: Print Out the Comic Strip

We recommend that each comic strip, once it is complete, be printed out. These hard copies indicate a "valuing" of student work. Once printed, the strips can be saved and uploaded to various websites, the class wiki, or a school website for sharing with parents, or as study and review materials.

How Do I Differentiate With Comic Life?

Like almost all tech tools, Comic Life lends itself to highly differentiated instruction. For students who struggle in writing, Comic Life may make writing assignments less intimidating. For some students, the teacher may assign them the development of only one or two sections of a comic strip. In other cases, when a written theme is required of some students in the class, the teacher can differentiate that assignment by having some students develop a written theme, while others use Comic Life to develop a comic covering the same content. For older students, a lesson stressing the similarities between storyboarding and outlining a writing assignment would help strengthen students' writing skills.

Students who are struggling in reading may feel more comfortable reading text that is supported by relevant pictures and drawings or other images. Those students can practice important literary skills on the comic strip itself before transferring those skills to larger reading assignments. The Common Core State Standards are likely to result in increased emphasis on the use of literature, as well nonfiction written assignments, and Comic Life accommodates this by providing students with opportunities to develop comic strip adaptations of important works of literature.

> For students who struggle in writing, Comic Life may make writing assignments less intimidating.

Comic Life also accommodates those students who are visually oriented, and these students often benefit from seeing the material presented in comic strip format in order to fully comprehend the content. However, the ability to produce original comic strip texts makes this tech tool appealing for linguistically strong students as well. When assigning projects, teachers should think through the students' learning styles and try to partner these types of strengths together so that one student is not threatened by either the visualization aspect of the assignment or by the writing requirements. Because today's learners are constantly surrounded by visual stimuli, using the visual stimuli provided within comics can certainly help students learn to visualize content material, a critical skill for our 21st century learners ("Using Comics," 2005).

> Because today's learners are constantly surrounded by visual stimuli, using the visual stimuli provided within comics can certainly help students learn to visualize content material, a critical skill for our 21st century learners.

Today, there are many graphic novel representations of classic texts available for students. Teachers in middle elementary or middle school classrooms may wish to have their students needing extra enrichment with the content material show how these graphic novels portray the classic text. Those learners could then create a comic strip for the text for use by others in the class. This provides students with the opportunity to analyze, synthesize, and then summarize the material for their peers. Teachers can then provide copies of these "mini-texts" as study guides to students who are having difficulty comprehending the text. Once these students begin to understand the text on their own, they can create their own visual representation of the content.

In this context, we should also mention that differentiation options may involve options on which tech tool the students use. For example, teachers may wish to provide some student choice by combining several tech tools for students to consider using for a given assignment. When assessing student understanding of a particular historical event, teachers may allow the students to choose between producing a podcast from that time period, creating a comic strip depicting the events, or putting together a Glog with the main ideas summarized. Giving students an opportunity to choose the medium that is most comfortable for them allows for differentiation and provides an opportunity for success in that student's area of strength. In that context, each student's understanding of the content can be easily analyzed by the teacher, and the students would not be threatened by the format of the assignment.

Extra Resources

A Sample Lesson Plan

Standard: Common Core State Standards—English Language Arts Reading, Literature for Grade 4: RL.4.2. Determine a theme of a story, drama, or poem from details in the text; summarize the text.

Students will . . .

- Reflect on literature read in class during the past nine weeks
- Determine the theme of the story they choose as their favorite and summarize the text
- Study how comic strips succinctly tell stories with visuals and concise text
- Use Comic Life to portray the most important details of the literature chosen and create their own comic

Materials

- Literature studied from past nine weeks
- Sample comics to study
- Digital cameras
- Comic Life software on computers

Preparation

- Purchase comic life subscription for at least two or three classroom computers
- Obtain use of digital camera (preferably three to five so that each small group can use one)
- Assemble props for students to use when depicting story
- Gather sample comics for students to analyze
- Create a list of literature read during the semester so that students can choose the piece of text they would like to summarize through Comic Life

Directions

- Pass out sample comic strips. Let students look through the strips and discuss the plot and summarize the comic. Discuss which components of the comic helped portray the story (pictures, facial expressions, speech bubbles).
- Place students in groups of three to five and have them choose one of the stories read throughout the semester to depict in a comic.
- Before creating the visual representation, have students choose the six to eight important components of the story that need to be included in the frames of the comic strip.
- Have students work in teams to take pictures that will portray their story. Students may need to use props found throughout the classroom and may create costumes to replicate characters.
- Students will then need time to take the pictures that will tell their story.
- Once students have their pictures, upload them onto Comic Life and allow students time to work on creating their story frames.
- Upload created comics onto class blogs and wikis. These short summaries can be used as review and can even be saved for the following group of students as intervention and study material.

Please note that this activity will most likely take three or more class periods to complete. Allow students plenty of time to create their comics and analyze their content.

Helpful Websites for Comic Life

Check out the following tabs on www.comiclife.com for more ways to integrate Comic Life into your classroom.

http://www.comiclife.com/education#teacheruse

The "Teacher Use" tab has ideas for general classroom use including class newsletters and creating class rules.

http://www.comiclife.com/education#language

Use the "Language" tab for ideas on how Comic Life can help your language arts lessons.

http://www.comiclife.com/education#history

The "History" tab has samples for how many history teachers use the features in Comic Life to bring the content material to life.

http://www.comiclife.com/education#mathematics

Comic Life allows students and teachers to create mathematics worksheets with the content material. This tab will explain how to create and use this feature in your classroom.

http://www.comiclife.com/education#science

The "Science" tab has specific examples of student work from science curriculum.

Conclusions

Like many of the other tech tools in this book, Comic Life builds on the desire of C2S2 students to learn visually. Also, comics are frequently associated with pleasurable pastime, and using that association to teach academic content can foster increased student attention. For subjects that lend themselves to pictures, we do recommend teachers explore this option.

References

Lyga, A. (2006). Graphic novels for (really) young readers. *School Library Journal*. Retrieved from http://www.schoollibraryjournal.com/article/CA6312463.html

Stillwell, T. (2011). Reading with pictures—supporting comics in the classroom. *Wired*. Retrieved from http://www.wired.com/geekdad/2011/02/reading-with-pictures-supporting-comics-in-the-classroom

Using comics and graphic novels in the classroom. (2005). *The Council Chronicle*. Retrieved from http://www.ncte.org/magazine/archives/122031

Tech Tool 15

Google Apps

What Do I Need to Know?

Google has developed a suite of comprehensive software programs for educational use, called *Google Apps*, and many school districts around the nation are beginning to implement this tool as they move into tech-based instruction (Owen, 2011; Richardson & Mancabelli, 2011). Information can be found online at http://www.google.com/apps/intl/en/edu/. A basic level of Google Apps is free for public schools, but that free option is limited to only ten user accounts. With larger numbers of students in the classroom, Google Apps is available for a fee of $50 per user per year, and while somewhat costly, this program has been widely adopted by schools in some areas. For example, by 2010, 50 of the 197 school districts in Oregon had begun to use Google Apps (Owen, 2011), and other Oregon districts were exploring this option.

Google Apps is a cloud-based suite of teaching tools, and thus, all work on Google Apps is stored on a Google server and is available to students both at school and at home. Student work is protected by a login procedure and a password (Bender & Waller, 2011; Richardson & Mancabelli, 2011). Thus, this program is as secure as any other online data, such as your personal bank account or any data stored on school district computers.

Rather than merely one teaching tool, Google Apps provides a number of tech tools, including many that have been described previously, and these tools can assist schools in moving toward tech-based instruction. These include

Gmail—allows schools to set up and offer free e-mails for all students and faculty;

168

Google calendar—a tool used for organizational purposes and communication between faculty, students and parents;

Google Sites—provides an option for developing blogs or wikis, including both document and video or photo hosting (see Tech Tools 3, 4, 5, and 8); and

Google Docs—a sophisticated word processing, editing and document sharing option that includes PowerPoint and a spreadsheet for student and teacher use (similar to Tech Tool 13—Scribd).

Definition: Google Apps is a cloud-based suite of teaching tools, including Gmail, Google calendar, Google sites for blogs and wiki development, and Google Docs for collaborative document development.

Of these software programs, Google Docs is perhaps the best known, as that software has been around for a while and has been used in many schools. It has long been recognized by educators that word processing and spreadsheets represent two of the most basic needs in education of the 21st century, and Google Docs offers them both

> Google Apps provides a number of programs that can assist schools in moving toward tech-based instruction.

for use in the classroom. Thus, Google Docs is an excellent resource for creating, editing, and sharing written content online, either individually or as a collaborative effort, and once again, collaborative development of ideas, using various technologies, will be one hallmark of 21st century classrooms, as well as 21st century workplaces. For more introductory information on using Google Docs in the classroom, teachers can check out a free guide (http://www.scribd.com/doc/88518869/Google-Docs-for-Teachers-2012).

How Do I Begin With Google Apps?

Step 1: Select a Google Apps Option

To use Google Apps, teachers should go to the website above, and create a free Google account and an account for each student. That process is not difficult, but teachers must select either the limited free option, though only ten users including both students and teachers can use that, or the fee-based subscription. The free option, while it will not accommodate an entire class of students, might be useful in limited situations. For teachers who might be unfamiliar with cloud-based computing, this free starter package might be very appropriate. Also, in classes where many students already have e-mail accounts, teachers can use this free Google Apps option to develop Gmail accounts for students without e-mail. For getting an entire class into Google Apps, teachers will need to discuss this purchase with their administrator, since this cost for an average class (one teacher and twenty-five students) represents a yearly expenditure of $1,300.

Step 2: Create Student E-mail Accounts

The next step would be to set up e-mail accounts for all of the students within the program. Using accounts set up within Google Apps provides the option for some degree of educator monitoring of these e-mail accounts, and also delivers an e-mail option for students who may not have e-mail accounts elsewhere. Depending on the number of accounts to be created, teachers could allow students to do that or work with students as they did that task.

Step 3: Create a Wiki

As the next task, we recommend the creation of a wiki for the next unit of instruction to be covered. The guidelines for wiki creation (see Tech Tool 4) will help, but that software (wikispaces.com) and the wiki creation steps within Google Apps procedures may differ a bit; however, teachers who have created one or two wikis in one software package can, in most cases, navigate their way through a similar program with relative ease. If you are using Google Apps, we do recommend that you create your wiki using that tool rather than wikispaces, as described above. Wikis, when created in Google Apps, are referred to as *Google Sites* but the functions will be similar to the wikis previously described. These Google Sites can be set up so that anyone can edit the content, and these allow the teacher to record all changes and undo any unwanted edits.

Step 4: Create Documents for Collaborative Work

C2S2 students are expecting learning activities that involve significant collaboration, and Google Docs is particularly effective in that regard. In fact, rather than a wiki, teachers may wish to begin by creating a draft or outline of a document for students to complete within Google Docs. The initial document may be created by either the teacher or by students. Once the initial document is created and saved, teachers can send it to students for them to review and edit. Because of the cloud-based nature of this software program, any of the students or the teacher can get to the document and edit it at any time. Further, the teacher can determine which students are contributing to the development of the documents since all of the revisions are archived, and any of previous revisions of the document can be opened and explored as necessary. On collaborative assignments, the teacher can use this function to see which student made specific contributions to a document, and if necessary, revert back to a previous edition of the document.

Step 5: Upload Your Podcasts or Other Videos

Once your account is created, in addition to using the Google Docs functions, you can likewise upload podcasts from almost any source (this function is similar to Tech Tool 8—Jing). Of course, teachers should make only content-rich podcasts available for the students, and the level of content for each uploaded podcast or video should be carefully examined.

How Do I Differentiate Using Google Apps?

As shown in the example above, group work using Google Apps does present a variety of opportunities for students with different learning styles and preferences to contribute to completion of a video report or PowerPoint presentation. Linguistic learners will probably be somewhat more skilled at developing a storyboard for a video or PowerPoint presentation, whereas visually strong learners may be more adept at framing video shots as the project is developed. Of course, teachers should always encourage students to challenge themselves by attempting tasks that are not directly in line with their preferred modes of learning or learning styles. However, project assignments of this nature provide many more opportunities for differentiating learning than do more static, hard-copy-only assignments. In short, the differentiation options in the 21st century classroom are limited only by the imaginations of the teachers and students.

Further, student participation is quite likely to go up when collaborative, cloud-based tech tools are used. In fact, students have anecdotally reported that they are more likely to complete homework when it is collaborative in nature through these online programs, and they indicate that being able to write and edit the same document is "cool!" (Owen, 2011). Once again, the

> Student participation is quite likely to go up when collaborative, cloud-based tech tools are used.

expectations of C2S2 kids are quite obvious in that single word—"Cool!"

We do recommend that teachers allow a great deal of student choice in how collaborative assignments are completed. Of course, all students must be required to complete some of the work, in some fashion, but within that broad parameter, facilitating student choice is strongly encouraged, and these tech-based assignments provide many opportunities for students to make choices in how to complete their work.

Finally, a critical aspect of differentiated instruction has always been the fact that students can and do learn from each other as they work in small groups. In other words, in differentiated groups where group membership is based on the same general learning styles and preferences, students will be able to instruct each other, and they are likely to motivate each other toward mastery of the learning content. Clearly the types of collaborative work that can be fostered within these cloud-based, document creation and sharing programs will facilitate that critical aspect of differentiation.

Other Comprehensive Teaching Tools

While various news stories and the technology literature suggest that Google Apps is one of the more common cloud-based teaching applications (Owen, 2011), there are several other companies that provide an entire suite of educational tools similar to Google Apps that teachers may hear of. Some of these other programs are also freely available to teachers. For example, Microsoft Live has recently been developed by the Microsoft Corporation (Microsoft Live@edu) for teachers to use, and many of these same cloud-based functions are available in that program. Likewise, Open Office (OpenOffice.org) is an open-source site that provides similar, cloud-based educational tools. Various districts may choose to use these software platforms rather than Google Apps, and teachers should be aware of these options.

Conclusions

Given the size and frequency of use of this parent company Google, any free tool developed by this company will command immediate attention. Of all the tech tools presented herein, one might well expect this tool to garner more attention from educators because of the name recognition of Google. While many other combinations of tech tools can accomplish the same tasks, we do encourage teachers to become aware of this tool, and no one in education should be surprised if this is adapted within their school or school district as a tool for all teachers to use.

References

Bender, W. N., & Waller, L. (2011). *The teaching revolution: RTI, technology, and differentiation transform teaching for the 21st century.* Thousand Oaks, CA: Corwin.

Owen, W. (2011, October 3). Google Apps is the hottest thing in schools, but some parents worry about privacy. *The Oregonian.* Retrieved from http://www.coregonlive.com/washingtoncounty/index.ssf/2011/10/google_apps_is_the_hottest_thi.html

Richardson, W., & Mancabelli, R. (2011). *Personal learning networks: Using the power of connections to transform education.* Bloomington, IN: Solution Tree Press.

Tech Tool 16

Vokis, Avatars, and Animation!

What Do I Need to Know?

In discussing Tech Tool 14—Comic Life, we made the point earlier that visual representations grab students' attention. However, these graphic representations have an even stronger effect when the images actually represent the C2S2 students themselves! In fact, such animation activities are so powerful they could well be considered a universal language that has the ability to reach virtually all students, including students with varying backgrounds and academic strengths (Stansbury, 2012). In addition, allowing students to learn through animation lowers the intimidation aspect of a classroom environment and provides an avenue for learning in a nonthreatening environment. Finally, many teachers have reported that that students are more engaged and retain more content material when they are able to creatively express themselves through animation ("Detroit Schools," 2011).

Animation in the Classroom

With that noted, the thought of creating movies and animation can seem daunting to even a tech-savvy teacher, but there are tools available, such as *Voki*, that will help make animation a reality in the classroom. Voki is a free animation tool that allows students to create an avatar for themselves and use that in ongoing class research and discussion. Voki is one of the easiest animation programs to use (www.voki.com). It is a free service that allows a user to create a customized avatar, a character or graphical representation of the individual student that each student creates. In Voki, students create their own avatar and then write dialogue for their avatar to speak. Once created, these speaking avatars and that content can be posted on blogs and websites or shared through e-mail.

Definition: Voki is a free animation tool that allows students to create an avatar for themselves and use that in ongoing class research and discussion.

Although the most basic Voki service is free, this level of service is funded by ads which pop up on the site. In contrast, the next level of service, "Voki Classroom," is a subscription service available for educators. For around $2.50 a month, a teacher is given access to all standard Voki features as well as a system to manage vokis for the entire class. Once a teacher has purchased this level of service, he can create student accounts, manage assignments, receive unlimited tech support through the website, and set privacy settings to private. In this level of service, there are no ads displayed. We strongly recommend that teachers opt to use the Voki Classroom account for security and ease of use for each educator. An introductory video on Voki Classroom is available on YouTube (http://www.youtube.com/embed/ao9KQltMkP0), and we recommend that teachers view that video if they wish to consider using Voki.

Once you have created a classroom account in Voki, there are endless ways to integrate Voki animations into the classroom curriculum. Students can use their avatar for any type of oral report from book reviews to foreign language exams. Students can create avatars and scripts to practice writing persuasive arguments, present research findings, or introduce themselves at the beginning of the year. Like the other tech tools mentioned in the book,

Figure 16.1

Source: © 2012 Oddcast Inc.

these avatars can be uploaded to wikis and blogs, creating a catalog of review options for the end of the year. Students can access their peers' avatars to review content material throughout the year.

As part of the Voki Classroom, teachers can outline an assignment on the website for students to complete. Once they have completed their assignment with their avatar, the teacher can go online, access the avatar, evaluate the dialogue, and grade the project. Teachers will be able to manage several different classrooms on the account as well as different lessons and assignments. There is also a database for teachers to check out other educators' lesson plans using Voki (www.voki.com/lesson_plans.php), and those lesson plans can be searched by grade level and subject. In short, Voki is an excellent teaching tool and will serve virtually all teachers in each subject area.

> Voki is an excellent teaching tool and will serve virtually all teachers in each subject area.

Other Teaching Ideas Using Voki

There are many other creative ways to use animation and student-created avatars in the classroom. Here are just a few more ideas found throughout the Voki website (www.voki.com).

- *Use Student Avatars for Proofreading.* Have students create an avatar and then type their paper for their avatar to speak. Once the student hears their avatar speaking, they can read along. Students make corrections based on the avatar's speaking. For example, they might need to add a period, correct spelling, or rewrite the text to help the text flow. There is an excellent YouTube video available that presents this teaching option for second-through fourth-grade students using Voki avatars (http://www.youtube.com/embed/3O4rQXcBrp4). Teachers may wish to view that video to get additional ideas on using avatars in the classroom.
- *Use Introduction Avatars.* Have students create an avatar that introduces themselves to their classmates at the beginning of the year. This can assist shy students in their social integration into a new class.
- *Use Avatars for Recitation Assignments.* Many students can be shy about reciting their own written assignments, such as poems or stories. Teachers may wish to allow students to choose a poem and have their avatar recite it.

- *Use Avatars to Practice Reading Fluency.* Teachers might assist struggling students by letting students record themselves speaking a particular text and then analyze their own fluency rates. The avatars can even be used for additional practice or repeated readings of the same text.
- *Use Avatars to Develop Automaticity With Math Facts.* Teachers might assign a set of multiplication facts to be studied, and then encourage students to recite those facts using their avatar. These recitations can be uploaded to a class wiki so that there is a bank of facts for the entire class. Students can explain any tips and tricks that they know for their number.
- *Use Avatars to Represent Historical Figures.* Have students choose one figure from the historical period being studied and have them use an avatar to explain why that historical figure acted as he did (Continental Congress members, civil rights leaders, etc.).

As this list indicates, this tech tool can be used in a wide variety of ways in various subject areas. Teachers and students together are likely to find additional uses for the avatars that represent each student.

How Do I Get Started With Voki?

Step 1: Complete One or Two Tutorials

At the Voki website (www.voki.com), a wide variety of tutorials is available to help you get started. Some of these were created by teachers using Voki (for example, check out the video tutorial at http://www.youtube.com/embed/3O4rQXcBrp4). We recommend that teachers spend thirty to forty-five minutes using one or more of those initially, and then create an avatar for themselves. This will help the teacher understand the process and how these student avatars may be used in the classroom.

Step 2: Select Your Voki Service

While various options, including a free option, are available, we recommend the Voki Classroom fee-based service, which is $29.95 per year (or $2.50 monthly) for one class. Of course, you may wish to experiment with the free service for a while prior to jumping into the subscription service. If you are opting for the subscription service, you merely go to the Voki website (www.voki.com) and search for the "Get Voki Classroom." Follow the steps on the website to sign up—you will need to give your name, e-mail, and create a password. You can opt to sign up for two years and receive a pricing that lowers the cost to $1.87 a month.

Step 3: Create an Avatar

Once you have signed up for either program, you will be able to create an avatar. We do recommend that teachers go through this process first, but this website is user-friendly and does not require much explanation for creating Voki avatars. Students as young as first grade have successfully created their own avatars. When you are ready to create a new Voki avatar, you will need to decide on four basic things including the avatar's style, look (customization), voice, and background.

Step 4: Modify or Tweak The Look of the Avatar

Students will have options when creating avatars to make their character an animal, "edgy," "oddball," VIP, and more. Once they have chosen a character, they can change the character's clothing, hair, and mouth style, and even add accessories. Students can change (or tweak) the color of the character's eyes, hair, skin, and mouth to create the final look of their avatar. We do recommend setting a time limit for this part of the students' assignment as it can be quite time consuming going through all of the various options and styles, and you will want students to have time to work on the actual assignment after they complete the creation of their avatar.

Step 5: Select a Background

Students next need to choose a background for the avatar. It can be helpful to discuss theme and content with students. If they are creating an avatar for an oral report in a foreign language, have them create an avatar and select a background that resembles the chosen culture. If they are creating an avatar that is depicting a particular historical event, have them customize the avatar and background appropriately. Thinking about and using appropriate customization will give students that much more time with the content material and its applications.

Step 6: Select a "Voice" Option

There are four options for giving the avatar a voice. Students can call in to the website and record their voice through the phone; type text and it will turn the text into speech; speak into a microphone; or upload an audio file.

Typing in text might be faster, but using a student's actual voice can be quite motivating.

Step 7: Create Content for the Avatar

After a voice option is selected, students will need to create the content for that avatar to present. This is the stage at which content can be introduced. Students can create a dialogue that is focused on the learning content, and upload that dialogue such that the avatar will present it, using a speaking voice.

Step 8: Save and Publish the Avatar

When a student has finished an avatar, they need to publish it. The student will simply click "Publish" and the website will provide the teacher and student a code that can be e-mailed or uploaded to a class blog or wiki. Once the avatar has been reviewed by the teacher, uploading the avatars to other websites is an easy process. These student-created avatars can also be set to private, such that only the student and teacher can see them.

How Do I Differentiate With Voki?

Voki creates many avenues for differentiating instruction. One obvious option is differentiation of student presentations. For students who are intimidated by presenting in front of the class, a fear often resulting from fear of negative feedback or a general lack of self-confidence, class presentations can be done through their avatar. Even very shy students now have the ability to present in front of their peers, via their avatar. Voki avatars take the pressure off the speaking portion of the assignment and allow those students to focus on the content material and creation of their final presentation.

Teachers can also vary the Voki creation assignment to accommodate various learning styles and student strengths. Students struggling in content material may only be required to create a relatively simple, thirty-second avatar presentation, while those students needing extra enrichment may be required to cover more content, in depth, and develop a ninety-second presentation, which is the maximum time allocated via this website.

Since avatars can be uploaded to class websites or wikis, higher-level students can create "peer tutor" avatars for other students. These advanced students can create avatars that explain particular components of a mathematics problem, a science formula, or any other content material for their peers. Further, this is excellent teaching for both the advanced students and the students with more learning challenges, since the skills associated with synthesizing content material and explaining that material give the tutors more time to analyze the material. Once the avatars are uploaded to class blogs, the students who needed that intervention would access the avatars and get clarification on concepts exactly when such clarification is needed. Again, they are able to access these avatars and hear the review material and never have to fear asking the questions in class.

Student avatars can even assist in formative assessment on a one-to-one basis. Those students needing extra intervention might be required to create avatars to help them review the content material and think through the concepts that are causing confusion. In that content, they would create the dialogue for their avatar to use in explaining the concept. Once that content is uploaded, the teacher can access the avatar, listen to the student's explanation, and find the areas where the student needs extra help. This process, again, allows the student to receive individualized help in a nonthreatening environment.

Finally, using avatars as part of the teacher presentation also helps differentiate for various learning styles. Students who are more visually oriented will benefit from being able to see the avatar versus simply listening to a podcast or hearing a teacher discuss the problem or content. These teacher created avatars can also be loaded onto blogs or wikis so that students can access them at a later date, both in class and at home, for review.

Other Resources for Your Classroom

A Sample Lesson Plan

Standard: Common Core State Standards—Reading Standards for Literature K–5, Grade 4: RL.4.3

Describe in depth a character, setting, or event, in a story or drama, drawing on specific details in the text (e.g., a character's thoughts, words, or actions).

Students will . . .

- Select a particular character from the text read in class
- Analyze the character's thoughts and actions in the text

- Create an avatar that represents the chosen character
- Have the avatar explain the character's actions in the text—why did the character do what he/she did? What prompted the actions? What was the character feeling throughout the text?
- Cite examples from the text to validate the avatar's explanation

Materials

- Access to class text
- Computers with access to Internet
- Voki Classroom subscriptions

Preparation

- Download and create classroom management on Voki Classroom
- Write assignment and create lesson page for students to access project
- Read class text and help students choose character for analysis

Directions

- After completing a class text, have students choose one character from the story for analysis.
- Explain that students will need to think through the text and explain why the character did what he/she did in the text? What examples from the text prove their analysis?
- Students first need to write a dialogue for their avatar analyzing the character's thoughts, feelings, and actions.
- Once the teacher has approved the dialogue, students access the Voki Classroom page and create their avatar.
- After teacher approval, upload avatars to class blogs and have students compare their analysis of characters.
- Keep avatars on the blog for continual review of that particular text.

Extension

- Have students "continue" the story by letting their avatar explain the rest of the story and what would happen if the story continued.
- Have students create an avatar that explains whether or not they agree with the character's decisions in the text.

Beyond Avatars! Animation Options for the Classroom!

There are a variety of websites that offer more extensive animation options for teachers (TEEContributor, 2011). We recommend that teachers initially use the Voki option, and then, as their expertise increases over time, that they explore some of the more advanced options below. While some free versions of these sites allow one to create an animation, most charge a nominal fee. However, if a teacher in your school is already using one of these websites for animation, then by all means, partner with that teacher and explore that website first!

ABCya.com

ABCya.com is a free gaming website for young children that provides games and apps for use under the guidance of parents and teachers. No personal information is collected at this site. This is one of the best animation sites for young users (TEEContributor, 2011). Here, students can draw pictures in frames and present them in sequence.

DoInk.com

This website allows students of various ages to create an animation and then clone it to place it in a sequence of scenes. Thus, this is a great site for creation of larger project-based learning assignments focused on specific content.

GoAnimate.com

This website is appropriate for middle and high school learners, and many teachers use this to create animated videos for teaching purposes. The site provides various lesson plans that can be explored. This tool also provides the option on comic strip creation, and the site is relatively easy to use.

Conclusions

Animation can bring educational content to life, and C2S2 students are used to using avatars in their games. Again, because of the habits of today's generation of learners, teachers can anticipate higher engagement when using Vokis for teaching in the class, and having some animation tools will enrich almost every classroom.

References

Detroit schools choose movie maker to fuel creativity and boost test scores. (2011, August 29). *eSchoolNews*. Retrieved from http://www.eschoolnews.com/2011/08/29/detroit-schools -choose-movie-maker-to-fuel-creativity-and-boost-test-scores

Stansbury, M. (2012, February 10). Six ed-tech resources for ELL/ESL instruction. *eSchool News*. Retrieved from http://www.eschoolnews.com/2012/02/10/six-ed-tech-resources-for-ellesl -instruction/2/?

TEEContributor. (2011). *7 Web 2.0 animation tools*. Retrieved from http://h30411.www3.hp.com/ posts/1045052-7_Web_2_0_animation_tools?mcid=Twitter

Tech Tool 17

Vlogs

What Do I Need to Know?

The students today, students that we refer to as C2S2 students, are used to video demonstrations and content, and when that can be coupled with other media, the power for learning is virtually unlimited. We have mentioned previously the instructional power that results from combining several tech tools into one format in order to capitalize on C2S2 students' interest in learning from a variety of audio and video sources. Imagine a tech tool that can ultimately serve students who are (a) linguistically strong and want to write, (b) need visual representation, or (c) work best with auditory stimulation. *Vlogging* takes the best attributes of podcasts and blogs and combines them into one medium for instruction—video logs.

A *vlog* is a video blog where each entry is posted as a video instead of text, as in a traditional blog (see Tech Tool 3—Blogs). Vlogs are more extensive than individual instructional videos of the type that might be posted on YouTube or TeacherTube, in that vlogs typically include a series of videos grouped around the topic under study. Over time, these may even be scaffolded so that later vlog entries present higher-order content than previous vlog entries. Similar to blogs, vlogs are updated regularly and are archived by date. Vlogs, again like blogs, are interactive in nature, and users can subscribe to a vlog for updates and then leave comments about the various vlog entries.

> **Definition:** A vlog is a video blog where each entry is posted as a video instead of text.

There is not a lot of discussion on using vlogs in education, as this is a newer medium for student learning, and yet there are numerous benefits for use in the classroom. One undeniable advantage of using video in the classroom is that students have the ability to access the material again and again (Branigan, 2005), and that is further enhanced by the cloud-based nature of vlogs. When a short vlog entry is created about content material, that material is made available to students after the school day ends, which gives them ample time to work through new concepts. This is one of the strengths of the Khan Academy (see Tech Tool 6), and availability of video instruction is the basis of the flipped classroom concept discussed previously.

Students are comfortable with video as an instructional medium; in fact, they seem to prefer it! Video is a medium that excites and motivates students today, and students are using this tool themselves frequently. Consider the statistics from YouTube that four billion videos are viewed per day and one hour of video is uploaded to YouTube every second (www.youttube.com). In the year 2011, YouTube had one trillion views which equates roughly one hundred forty views per person on Earth. Over seven hundred YouTube videos are shared on Twitter each minute (www.youtube.com). Video is clearly an integral part of our students' daily lives and as educators; we would be remiss if we do not use this powerful medium, both at home and in the classroom. In a broader sense, it is vital that we join in with our students and teach these new media literacies which involve new text formats along with digital video and other new media technologies (Barone & Wright, 2008). A commitment to teaching and integrating these new literacies in the classrooms ensures equal opportunity for all students (Barone & Wright, 2008).

Creating a vlog can be an excellent instructional endeavor for students to undertake. It may seem overwhelming to try and constantly post new video entries for a classroom vlog, but having students take responsibility for the vlog upkeep gives them an opportunity to take ownership in the project and will focus them on the content. One option is to create a daily review vlog where one student each day posts a two- or three-minute summary of the work done in class. This type of vlog would be an invaluable resource for many people, including absent students, interested parents, students who wish to review content, and curious administrators. Having the students discern the most important parts of the day and succinctly share them via the video post gives them an opportunity to analyze the material and synthesize the content under study in their own words. As with other tech tools described in the book, this archived list of video entries creates a study guide that can be used year after year.

We should emphasize that vlogs of this nature can also build strong connections with families, and that is always a concern among educators. Video posts can document student presentations, give tours of the classroom, and highlight important aspects of field trips. Teachers can create posts as well and use the vlog as a way to introduce themselves or to promote upcoming events. We do recommend that teachers using vlogs invite family members to join in and view the vlog entries.

How Do I Get Started With Vlogs?

Step 1: Three Necessities for Vlogging

Teachers can undertake vlogging based on three necessities. These include the following:

1. *A digital video camera.* iPads, for example, include a camera, as do many computers. Also, many smartphones provide that option. An inexpensive handheld video camera will also work.
2. *Editing software.* Teachers can use some type of relatively simple video editing system, one of which is available on most modern computers—Windows Movie Maker. However, video editing software is not required when uploading videos.
3. *A hosting location.* Teachers will need to identify a location for posting the video entries for the vlog, and free options include YouTube or TeacherTube or blogging servers. Other free posting options include school websites and class wikis.

Step 2: Identify Your Video Tech Options

Creating a vlog is a simple process, particularly if you are familiar with writing your own blog. There are multiple ways to create a vlog—with a webcam and microphone on your computer, using a tablet such as an iPad that also includes this component, or by uploading your own videos from a handheld video camera. For educational use, we recommend a separate camcorder so that activities away from the classroom environment can be recorded. Using a webcam that is mounted to a computer tends to limit the videos to talking headshots taken at the computer desk, and while tablets are a bit more versatile, they are still a bit more cumbersome than a video camcorder, which can be used to film activities anywhere on or off the school campus.

Step 3: Editing Options in Vlogs

As teachers record vlog entries, they may wish to edit these, and depending on how a vlog video is created, editing the video after the fact might be an option. If a camcorder is used to create the video, Windows Movie Maker (which is a simple editing tool available on many computers today) might be one editing option. In general, we recommend that teachers forgo large video-editing jobs, until and unless they are fairly fluent in usage of video-editing software.

Step 4: Consider Student Security Prior to Posting a Vlog Entry

Once the video has been recorded and edited, teachers should immediately upload the file onto the hard drive and save it so it can be easily located. At that point, some consideration should be given to the vlog hosting location. This is critical for student security, particularly for very young students. Rather than merely posting vlog entries on public sites such as YouTube, vlogs can be posted on any typical blogging website, and a variety of blog hosting options were presented earlier in this book (see Tech Tool 3). Using a blogger service helps with security as most services offer privacy options. Since students will be videoing themselves and might video their surroundings (and inadvertently provide hints on their personal location), we recommend using a secure site and creating a vlog that is password protected. Those practices will keep the videos from being visible to the public on the World Wide Web.

With that student-security caution stated, many teachers are using video sharing websites such as YouTube or Vimeo to showcase their vlogs. We recommend using a secure blogging host in the classroom to create a vlog so that a password or login is required. There are numerous options for blogging hosts, but teachers should look for one that is ad-free and offers levels of security for students.

One blogging host that offers themes specifically for vlogging is WordPress (www.wordpress.com). Themes, such as "On Demand" and "Selecta," are optimized to showcase videos. Typically, these themes have larger playing windows for videos and the home page puts attention on the featured clip.

Whether you choose a site specifically for videos or not, each blog host varies slightly in set-up, so once a blog host is chosen, we recommend that you watch the tutorial videos and follow the step-by-step process delineated there for complete set-up. Most blogging hosts will require teachers to enter basic information such as name, e-mail information, and desired level of security. From there, templates are typically provided so that all is required is to point and click when posting.

Step 5: Video Creation

The biggest difference between a blog and a vlog is the obvious one; instead of starting a new text post as you would for a blog, the vlog means that you will create a new video entry. Still, these often work together, and most blogging sites have a video icon that allows you to upload your video directly onto the site. Essentially, when users accesses your vlog, they will see archived videos instead of archived text entries.

How Do I Differentiate With Vlogs?

Teachers have the opportunity to differentiate in three areas of the classroom—the content presented, the instructional process, or the product that is required of the student (Tomlinson, 2000), and like many tech-tool teaching options, a vlog provides opportunities for teachers to differentiate in all three areas. For example, teachers often have limited time in the classroom to cover the basic required content material and are frequently left with little or no time for intervention or enrichment. By creating a vlog, the teacher has ample time to do small videos that offer further explanation for students needing extra help and also create videos that take the content material to a higher level for those students needing enrichment. Thus, vlog entries can help differentiate the content.

As with other tech tools, vlogging extends the school day and allows students to access content material long after they leave the school building. A math teacher starting a unit on logarithms may create a vlog that shows several more detailed problems solved for students who left the classroom with a bit of confusion. The same teacher may then create a video post explaining how these logarithms may be used in the workplace for those students who understand the steps but question the reasoning behind learning the process.

This same idea applies when deciding how to differentiate the instructional process. By varying the learning activities that accompany the content material based on individual student needs, teachers are able to reach students at their own level, using a presentation style that easily matches the learner's preferred learning style. Offering various activities for students to complete also allows students to manipulate the concepts and ideas in a nonthreatening environment. Vlogs provide an opportunity to vary the process for each individual student.

Consider the math teacher working on logarithms; after presenting the unit, he may wish to have students explain in their own words the steps involved in solving the problems. Having the students summarize the steps ensures they are able to handle the problem and think through the appropriate actions independently. Instead of asking each student to write out the steps involved in solving the problem, the teacher is able to differentiate the process and product and offer several learning activities to ensure that each student is competent in the subject matter. The teacher may allow students to choose between writing out the steps involved, creating a vlog post explaining the steps, or even using Jing (see Tech Tool 8) to record the audio of the steps taken as they are displayed on the computer screen. Varying the learning activities and the product required gives students a sense of responsibility and freedom while at the same time allowing for thorough investigation of each student's understanding. Knowing how to utilize vlogs in the classroom gives you one more tool for differentiation in each lesson.

Other Resources and Ideas for Vlogs

Instructional Ideas Using Vlogs

Because vlogs basically involve video presentations, a vlog may not be the most appropriate medium for an entire lesson plan. However, vlogs are certainly well-suited for facilitating school-home connections, evaluations, informal assessments, and learning activities. Below is a list of ways that you may utilize vlogs in your classroom.

- Create a vlog post to introduce yourself to your students and parents. Have each student create a vlog introducing himself to his classmates.
- Create a review blog where each student takes turns summarizing the day's lesson.
- Create vlog entries documenting school events, presentations, and field trips.
- Record lessons and post them on the vlog for students' referral when working on homework.
- Have students practice fluency by recording themselves reciting a poem. Upload onto the class vlog for peer feedback.
- Have students interview community stakeholders with various jobs in the community and post those video interviews to the vlog. Encourage them to discover ways that the content being learned in class is utilized in the work force.
- Place students in small groups and have them act out text that is under study (either fictional or historical). Place the reenactments on the class vlog as additional study material.

- Video student discussions and small-group discussion and upload them onto the vlog. This allows all students to ultimately participate in each small-group discussion.
- Choose a current community event and have students debate the issues involved. Have students write a persuasive argument defending their opinion and then video that speech for the class vlog. Students can access and comment their peers' speeches agreeing or disagreeing with the vlogger's opinion.

Conclusions

Using video logs in the classroom will enrich the content, and like many of the visually oriented tech tools discussed here, vlogs are likely to increase student participation. While some students today might consider blogging somewhat "old school," vlogs are likely to be perceived as more modern by C2S2 students, and teachers should explore this relatively simple instructional option.

References

Barone, D., & Wright, T. E. (2008, December). Literacy instruction with digital and media technologies. *The Reading Teacher, 62*(4). Retrieved from http://www.readingrockets.org/article/29126

Brunlyun, C. (2005, June 1). Video goes to school, Part 3. *eSchool News.* Retrieved from http://www.eschoolnews.com/2005/06/01/video-goes-to-school-part-3

Tomlinson, C. A. (2000, August). Differentiation of instruction in the elementary grades. *ERIC Digest.* Retrieved from http://www.readingrockets.org/article/263/http://www.readingrockets.org/article/263

Tech Tool 18

Animoto

What Do I Need to Know?

As discussed in the previous section on vlogs, viewing photos and videos is, in the 21st century, a natural part of students' lives. The C2S2 students in our classes today expect to be able to view exactly what is going on with their peers, based on today's digital photography options and combined with modern social networking tools. Students, as well as their parents, use their digital cameras (either on their cell phones or their iPads), to keep up with each other, to know what is going on in the community, and to gather information about any topic they choose. Thus, one's ability to not only hear about but to actually see current activities creates connections between students and builds interest in various endeavors. As educators today, we have the ability to connect with our students, families, and key community stakeholders using the mediums they are used to, comfortable with, and have come to expect. Using video in the classroom can increase student engagement and motivation because video captures students' attention more easily than traditional modes of instruction (Branigan, 2005a). Further, video examples take abstract content and make it clear and tangible through visual representation (Branigan, 2005a, 2005b).

Vlogs or Video Presentations?

Of course, any teacher using vlogs or other tech tools mentioned in previous sections has the ability to upload pictures or short video clips. However, while vlogs can build on this seemingly innate desire for video examples, another tool for teachers to consider is *Animoto* (Branigan, 2005a). Animoto is a free service that takes these pictures a step further and allows teachers to create a professional-quality video presentation to be used in class. Animoto is user-friendly and requires only that you upload your photos and videos and this site will then create a completely orchestrated video presentation and set that presentation to music. The videos produced are three to four minutes in length, which is long enough to instruct but not so long that students lose interest or are unable to retain the content (Branigan, 2005a). Animoto differs from a vlog in that Animoto is typically used when teachers wish to have a stand-alone video on a particular topic and to use photos and text that already exist. Vlogs, in contrast, are a sequence of different video entries (i.e., a video log, see Tech Tool 17) on the same topic.

> **Definition:** Animoto is an online service that takes pictures a step further and allows teachers to create a professional-quality video presentation that can then be uploaded to class wikis, websites, or even YouTube.

Animoto videos may be used with students, parents, or other professionals. In a matter of minutes, teachers can create a high-quality presentation that gives parents, administrators, and community stakeholders a glimpse into their classroom (Bender & Waller, 2011). For example, if a class took a field trip to the local zoo, instead of just writing about the field trip in the monthly classroom newsletter, a teacher can take pictures and video while on the trip and create an Animoto presentation for the parents to view. In many ways, Animoto may be more user-friendly than creating a vlog entry; Animoto merely requires that the teacher or students take pictures (although video clips can also be uploaded), while the teacher and the class are actually in the zoo. Once the class returns to school, Animoto may be used to collect all of the class pictures and short video clips and put them into a nicely developed video. Text and music can be added at that point to enrich the video for instructional purposes. Allowing parents to view the Animoto video provides them with a clear understanding of where their child went, what she saw, and ultimately what she learned. Even better than uploading individual pictures that the teacher takes, Animoto allows the children themselves to use digital cameras to document the trip from their perspective. It can be quite surprising to teachers and parents to see what the students themselves see as relevant and interesting information.

Available Plans and Options

Animoto offers three basic plans for membership. The Animoto "lite" plan is free but only allows users to produce thirty-second videos. The Animoto

Figure 18.1

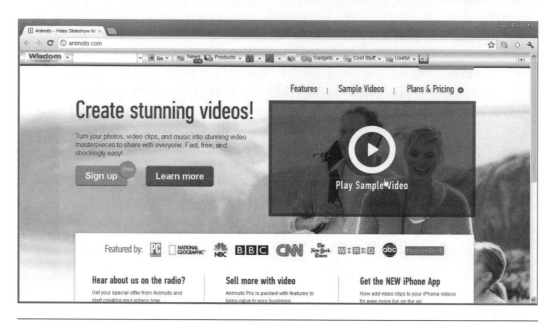

Source: © 2012 Animoto Productions

"plus" plan requires an annual payment of $30 but allows users to create limitless full-length videos that can be downloaded onto a computer or DVD. The Animoto "pro" membership is $249 yearly, and it allows for the creation of full-length videos with exclusive pro styles. For most teachers, we recommend the plus plan because videos created in that plan look and feel "professional" but do not come with the higher price tag.

There is also an option for educators to apply for a free Animoto education account which is the Animoto Plus-level account. We recommend that teachers visit the Animoto website (http://animoto.com/account/education/apply) and apply, by providing your name, e-mail, your school's name, and the grades you teach. Applications for free education accounts are processed in the order they are received, so it may take you a few days to hear back from the company. You will receive a confirmation e-mail that includes your code for the free account as well as a classroom code to allow your students to participate. The classroom code also allows your students to have free private accounts. However, that classroom code will expire after six months, so you will need to continually reapply for new codes through the same link mentioned above.

This is a great Web 2.0 teaching tool, because having students participate in the creation process offers great benefits for the retention of content material. Teachers can have students create videos as either a class project or as an authentic assessment, and both will require students to interact more intimately with content material they are learning as they record and edit their own videos (Branigan, 2005a, 2005b). No matter which way a teacher chooses to utilize this instructional tool, Animoto has the ability to increase both students' motivation and class participation. Further, teachers using Animoto videos in the classroom report that video assignments motivate students to not only participate but ultimately go beyond what is even expected of them in the learning process (Branigan, 2005b).

Sharing Animoto Presentations

Animoto offers various avenues for sharing the video once created. Teachers can upload their Animoto videos onto Facebook, YouTube, or a class wiki, making it easy to fit Animoto with other tech tools that are currently being used in the classroom. Videos can also be sent out through e-mail if teachers need to share with community stakeholders or the administration. The flexibility in sharing options accommodates schools that may have stricter policies when it comes to using social media and other tech tools.

The latest addition is the ability to create Animoto videos directly from an iPhone. Teachers can now download an Animoto app to their iPhone and create a video directly from their phone using images and videos previously on the iPhone. Ultimately, Animoto creates a professional product in a user-friendly, efficient manner, and the Animoto videos create a connected community of invested, highly motivated learners.

How Do I Get Started With Animoto?

Step 1: Creating a Teacher Account

Getting started with Animoto is quick and easy. Teachers need only visit the website (www.animoto.com) and provide their e-mail addresses. The company does not send out junk e-mail, but it does use your e-mail as your sign-in. The Animoto site will also e-mail you when your videos have finished processing.

Step 2: Choose Video Background and Photo Content

Once you have successfully created an Animoto account, you can start producing videos. The first step in the process is to choose a video background or theme. This is the backdrop for your video, and there are a variety of styles to choose from. Once you have selected your theme style, click the "Upload" button and the website will walk you through adding video and clips from your laptop, iPhone, iPad, or other personal computing device. You can also upload photos from a number of photo sharing sites including Flickr, Picasa, SmugMug, or Facebook.

Step 3: Sequence the Images

Once you have uploaded the pictures, you can arrange them in the order you would like for them to appear by simply clicking and dragging the pictures on the screen. This allows you to sequence the photos or video images to "tell the story" you wish to emphasize. You can also edit the videos if you like. The ideal time length for any single video clip is less than ten seconds, and the Animoto program allows you to edit your videos to find the perfect segment to showcase. You can add in text boxes to explain any videos or images at this point.

Step 4: Add Music

Once the pictures, videos, and text have been uploaded and ordered, you should pick a song to add as background music for your presentation. There is a library of over thirteen music genres for teachers to choose from, or you can upload your own MP3 audio track. For videos used only by your classroom, which are not for sale, there is typically no copyright problem using popular music. When creating the video, Animoto automatically adjusts the rate of rotation among your pictures and videos to match the tempo of the music, a feature which will add to the overall professionalism of your final video product.

Step 5: Add Limited Text

The Animoto program is not equipped to allow for adding text, but some teachers have figured out how to add a limited amount of text to the Animoto presentation, and this addition can increase the educational value of the final work. Teachers (or students) can add some text to a PowerPoint slide and then add that slide at the appropriate spot in the presentation.

Step 6: Create and Edit the Video

After choosing a background, uploading your media, creating text slides, as needed, and selecting a song, you are ready to tell the Animoto site to produce your video. Animoto will take your input, create a video, and send you an e-mail when it is finished. The creation process takes anywhere from ten to twenty minutes, and after that time, you can watch your finished video. Options are available for you to go back into the original storyboard template for the video and edit the video if needed.

All of the videos you create will be stored in your account. From your account page, you have the option to share your video via Facebook, Twitter, MySpace, Blogger, WordPress, and other similar sites. You can also share the link to your video by copying and pasting the code provided by Animoto. Animoto also allows you to e-mail directly from the creation space by entering in recipients' e-mail addresses. There is also a download option that allows you to store the finished video file directly onto the hard drive of your computer, and that allows you to use that video in your class again next year, if appropriate.

Step 7: Creating Student Accounts

If you applied and received the free educators account, you have the option to set up accounts for your students so that they can also create videos, and we do recommend this, since student creation is the hallmark, not only of Web 2.0 teaching tools, but of every 21st century classroom! You will need to either allow your students to use their own e-mail addresses coupled with the account code you were given by Animoto, or you can follow the directions to set up dummy accounts for your students (see http://help.animoto.com/entries/104077-how-do-i-set-up-accounts-for-my-students).

Any activity under the account will be sent to your original e-mail address when using dummy e-mail accounts for the students. Setting up dummy accounts will take a few more minutes of your time, but we strongly recommend that you use this set-up method, as it allows you to monitor all student activity. If students use their own e-mails, you will not be notified of activity on the account. When using Animoto for education, all videos will be set to private, and the only way that someone outside your class can view the video is if it has been officially shared through the video's link or if they are posted on another website, such as Facebook, for example.

How Do I Differentiate Instruction Using Animoto?

There are so many uses for Animoto, it seems that it would be more beneficial to brainstorm a variety of uses as opposed to listing one specific lesson plan. Of course, once a video is created, that video would not vary in content, though questions that students may be required to answer based on viewing that video could allow teachers to use Animoto videos in differentiated instructional activities. Here are a few additional ideas for classroom use for Animoto (also see http://teachweb2.wikispaces.com/Animoto):

- Create documentaries of class field trips to use in review activities.
- Require students to create their own class trip documentaries as part of a field trip follow-up assessment.
- Film and take still shots of students working on a project throughout a particular unit as well as their final presentations.
- Create video as a documentary of student work on projects for parents to review.
- Upload Animoto presentations onto your class blog so that students can review the material at the end of the year.
- Allow students to check out digital cameras and camcorders in order to create an "about me" video for the beginning of the year to create classroom community. Teachers should be sure to create one too!
- Have your students create a video detailing class expectations, routines, and perhaps include a tour of the school building.
- Provide those class expectation and school tour videos to new students, particularly ELL students and others with learning challenges, in order to help them become acclimated to their new environment.
- Have students go on scavenger hunts for particular examples of content material. For example, when studying various shapes in math class, have students go on a shape scavenger hunt and capture images and videos of shapes seen in their surroundings. Upload the photos and videos to create professional presentations that show how the math is applicable to their everyday life.
- Use images from the Internet to create a presentation that introduces content material for your students. If you are studying plants, create an introductory video cataloging the plants you will be studying. This can even be used for early elementary students by introducing a new letter sound with a video of pictures that begin with that sound.
- Create virtual field trips. If you do not have the funds to take a field trip, which is certainly a reality in many schools, teachers can create a virtual field trip through Animoto. In fact, teachers and students may upload images and clips they find on the Internet to take students anywhere in the world ("Virtual Field Trip," 2012).
- Have students collect pictures and short clips about a certain topic and create an Animoto presentation. Once the presentation is complete, have students switch Animoto presentations and write a creative piece about the images collected by one of their peers.

Conclusions

Animoto is a great way to use existing video and pictures to enrich the academic content, and C2S2 students respond well to learning via images. Once video clips are developed using this tool, teachers can use those repeatedly in various classes as well as in future years. This is a tech tool for teachers to consider, though we generally recommend that teachers should find one video-focused tech tool and master it prior to attempting to use various tools.

References

Bender, W. N., & Waller, L. (2011). *The teaching revolution: RTI, technology, and differentiation transform teaching for the 21st century.* Thousand Oaks, CA: Corwin.

Branigan, C. (2005a). Video goes to school, Part 1. *eSchool News.* Retrieved from http://www.eschoolnews.com/2005/04/01/video-goes-to-school-part-i

Branigan, C. (2005b). Video goes to school, Part 3. *eSchool News.* Retrieved from http://www.eschoolnews.com/2005/06/01/video-goes-to-school-part-3

Virtual field trip to help teach the history of immigration in America. (2012, March 21). *eSchool News.* Retrieved from http://www.eschoolnews.com/2012/03/21/virtual-field-trip-to-help-teach-the-history-of-immigration-in-america

Part IV

Tools for Social Learning and Networking

Tech Tool 19

Facebook

What Do I Need To Know?

Facebook has become something of a cult phenomenon over the last decade, and in many schools it is difficult to find a middle grade or high school student who does not have a Facebook account. This fact alone testifies to the different learning expectations and desires of C2S2 students in our classes today. Facebook is currently the most popular social networking site used by students and adults worldwide to present information on themselves to the world. By 2012, over 900 million individuals worldwide had chosen this social medium to present information about themselves to the world, and even Hollywood had noticed this dramatic growth (Watters, 2011; Wilmarth, 2010). By early 2012, Facebook promised to become a force in world economic markets as it fostered one of the largest initial product offerings of stock on the way to becoming a very large, publicly traded company.

> **Definition:** Facebook is the most popular social networking site used by students and adults worldwide to present information on themselves to the world.

In Facebook, individuals who are thirteen years of age and have an e-mail account can establish an individual Facebook page on which they can post pictures of themselves or their activities, list their hobbies and interests, or simply post a written log (a few words to a paragraph) about their daily or hourly activities. Anyone else on Facebook can read those entries, if they search for and find the original user who posted the information. However, there are some controls that individuals can exercise to limit the information available about them (Phillips, 2011). In most cases, students (and many others worldwide) select a group of friends to share information with, and the phrase "friend me" has turned the noun *friend* into a verb! Thus, over time, Facebook participants develop a network of "followers" who access the information and can post back to each other's Facebook page. Postings may include text, photos, or brief videos, and again, the vast majority of Facebook users use it for socially networking with friends or family.

However, specifically because of the popularity of this social medium, many teachers in middle school and high school have begun to set Facebook pages for their students to use in class or at home (Ferriter, 2011; Ferriter & Garry, 2010; Watters, 2011). These educationally based Facebook pages are not primarily intended for social exchange; rather, these pages typically present information about the topic under study, including teacher's notes, reminders, or student-created posts on the topic of study (Anderson, 2012; Kessler, 2011; Phillips, 2011). In one example that was shared with the senior author of this text, a teacher in an Atlanta, Georgia, high school established a Facebook page related to her social studies class, specifically at the request of her students! It's an interesting and enlightening story, so here is what happened!

That teacher had previously encouraged students to use her cell phone number, on a very limited basis, and had encouraged her students to call her directly (and only) on the night before a unit test, to specifically address any content questions they had. She reported that she had received no calls at all before the first three unit assessments. After the third unit text, she asked why the students had not reached out to her with their questions as they studied the academic content on the night before the quiz. Their reply was enlightening! "We are all on Facebook. Can you just set up a Facebook page and let us contact you there?" Again, the expectations of today's C2S2 kids are quite apparent in that statement!

> When our students specifically request content-related communications via a specific communications option, shouldn't we, as educators, set up that communication tool?

In fact, this example demands a bit of a reality check among educators: When our students specifically request content-related communications via a specific communications option, shouldn't we, as educators, set up that communication tool? Because so very many students are using Facebook, it is clearly a preference for them. For that reason, it is advisable to consider this tech tool as one instructional option that teachers can use to "meet students where they are!"

Of course, the impressive power of using social networks to create learning networks is only now being explored, but the advantages of networking related to studying content cannot be overlooked. For example, one recently developed educational application has been devised for Facebook called *Hoot. me* (http://hoot.me/about/). This tool effectively connects students from the same school or class that happen to be studying the same content on a given evening (Watters, 2011). When a student gets online via Facebook, rather than ask the usual Facebook question, "What's on your mind?" the Hoot.me app prompts the student with the question, "What are you working on?" When students answer that question, they might be presented with the option to join a study session with other students from their class or their school related to that topic. In short, this application will seek out other students with a Facebook account from the same school or class who are likewise working on that topic (Watters, 2011), and then suggests that those students chat with each other about that academic content. Thus the application is effectively pairing students together for joint study opportunities.

How Do I Begin to Use Social Networks in Teaching?

Step 1: Investigate School Policies on Social Networking

While some teachers are using Facebook for instructional purposes (Anderson, 2012; Kessler, 2011; Phillips, 2011), others have identified various roadblocks to the use of any social networking site for instruction. First, many school districts currently have policies that specifically prohibit social networking among teachers and students, In the example of the Atlanta teacher described above, the school policy specifically prohibited use of Facebook with students, and the teacher above had to seek special permission to teach using Facebook.

Of course, we agree that it is clearly inappropriate for teachers to socialize with students on Facebook or to use any other 21st century communications tool for socializing with students. An appropriate use policy can help alleviate these concerns, and as an additional step, we recommend that when teachers choose to use Facebook for teaching the content in their class, they should always include an administrator from the school as a participant on that

Facebook page. This way, virtually all communications can be monitored, and both the teacher and the students are protected.

It may help with school policies if educators describe their use of social networks in teaching as "learning networks," which was recommended by Richardson and Mancabelli (2011). In that fashion, the teaching-learning process is stressed, and this may help alleviate some concerns on using social networks for teaching. On that basis, we advocate that teachers investigate the use of social networking sites in the context of their teaching. The principal's office is a good place to inquire initially, and many districts have teacher handbooks that address questions on using social networking sites as the basis for setting up learning networks focused on academic content.

> It may help with school policies if educators describe their use of social networks in teaching as "learning networks."

If such policies are entrenched, we can only assure teachers facing such policies that these are, in many cases, changing to address the education needs of 21st century learners, and if your district does not allow Facebook usage today in the classroom, that policy is likely to change soon, as more and more districts are considering the many appropriate uses of these social networking sites in education.

Step 2: Consider Ning, Edmodo, or Other Network Options

We advocate using Facebook and other social networking sites in education specifically because these sites are so popular with students. In fact, there are many advantages of using Facebook or other popular sites, not the least of which is that many students are already using these sites and are familiar with them. In that sense, teachers will not have to require that many students set up new accounts, since most already have a Facebook account. Further, teachers using Facebook or other commonly used social networking sites (see Tech Tool 20—Twitter or the sites described below) seem to be "with it" in the eyes of their students. In short, when students use modern technologies and teachers don't, the teachers lose some degree of credibility and do not seem as connected or as relevant in the 21st century world.

With those thoughts noted, there are social network alternatives that teachers might consider, and these may be somewhat less threatening from the perspective of parents in the community. For example, both *Edmodo* and *Ning* can provide the same learning networking options for students in your class, and depending on your community, neither of these may have negative parental concerns associated with them.

Edmodo is a free social networking option at which teachers and students can share information on the topic under study in a Facebook-type fashion (http://www.edmodo.com). Teachers can store links to relevant websites, digital files, assignments, and class calendars, and teachers and students alike can create and respond to information posted by others. After teachers create their free account, they invite their students to join. Students then sign up using a teacher-generated code that specifically assigns them to that teacher's class. Teachers can post to their class or privately to students (e.g., for awarding grades). Also, there is a set of reinforcement badges which teachers can award for student work.

Ning is a fee-based service that is currently being used by many educators (List & Bryant, 2009). Ning is the world's largest platform for creating social networks (http://www.ning.com) and was originally designed for business. It includes all of the options offered by Facebook and is relatively cheap to use. In particular, Ning Mini (see the website above) is a simple option for small social networks, such as an individual teacher's class, and originally cost $2.95 monthly. However, in 2010 Pearson Education, a large curriculum company, announced that they would partner with Ning to make these social networks free for teacher use. Those Ning Mini sites are limited to one hundred fifty persons, which should be enough for a teacher, her class, some administrators, and parents to join the network. Teachers need to visit the Pearson sign-up page to create a free Ning network (http://go.ning.com/pearsonsponsorship/).

While we discussed the advantages of using Facebook above, compared to these other social network options, there is one disadvantage to using Facebook in the classroom—the fact that so many kids are already using Facebook for personal communications. When students "friend" a teacher on Facebook, the teacher will see every post the student sends to his or her friends and family whether relevant to the class or not. Of course, various privacy settings can be manipulated to alleviate this concern, but that process can be cumbersome for many teachers and students. For this reason, many teachers who do use Facebook for teaching limit their use strictly to one-way communication. Thus, Facebook might become a platform in which teachers post information, pictures, digital files, or assignments, but students do not post any content. For this reason, use of social network options like Edmodo and Ning might be preferable, since those social networks can easily be limited to two-way contributions on class content, leaving the students' Facebook pages exclusively for private student use.

Step 3: Inform Parents

Parents have many fears associated with Internet usage, and educators must be quite sensitive to those fears. In fact, many fears are well-founded (e.g.,

> The parents should be assured that all Facebook communications for the class will be instructional in nature and that the teacher and school administrators will carefully monitor all Facebook comments.

the sexting epidemic among today's teenagers), and parents are only advocating for their child's safety. Once a teacher determines that a social network, such as Facebook, can be used in their school or district, the teacher should inform the parents about their intended use of that social network for school studies. The parents should be assured that all communications on the Facebook class site will be instructional in nature, and that the teacher and school administrators will carefully monitor all communications at that Facebook account. Also, in some cases, inviting parents to participate as "friends" can go a long way to alleviating parental concerns.

Step 4: Set Up A Teacher Account

Once school policy is determined and parents are informed of the new use of Facebook for educational purposes, the teacher is ready to begin using Facebook. Initially, teachers should go to the Facebook website (www.face book.com) and complete the application process. That website requires an e-mail address, and signing up for a Facebook account is fully explained at the site. The process for establishing Ning or Edomodo accounts is similar and is explained at these respective websites above.

Step 5: Investigate Potential Firewall Problems

In some cases, as teachers attempted to set up Facebook (or Ning or Edmodo) accounts using computers at school, they found that the set-up did not work, because of firewalls established by their school or school district. Many teachers have found that, even in schools that do not have provisions against social networks in the classroom, there may be a firewall prohibiting such usage.

A *firewall* is essentially an electronic block that is intended to prohibit access to specific sites (e.g., websites with inappropriate sexual content or vulgar language). Firewalls are often established by the technology person at the district

level, and sometimes are established at the specific instructions of the superinten-
dent. Of course, firewalls of that nature are established to prohibit teachers from
interacting with students in social network sites, since social networking is clearly
inappropriate in the teacher-student relationship. Thus, teachers might find that
they need to establish their Facebook account on a personal computer.

While protecting students is certainly a worthwhile goal, rather than
firewall blocks, we once again advocate an acceptable use policy as discussed
previously. While blocking some specific sites (e.g., sexual content sites, dat-
ing sites) is appropriate, firewalls can be bypassed. In fact, if you show these
authors a firewall, we can guarantee we'll show you a middle school student
in that district who can (and probably already has) get around it! Further,
blocking sites that can enrich education is clearly counterproductive. We've
personally worked in schools that block all social networking sites, not to
mention YouTube, TeacherTube, and many other websites that hold great
opportunities for educators.

Should such a firewall problem arise, we can only urge teachers to go the
extra mile and inquire about removing the firewall from certain sites, such as
Twitter, Facebook, YouTube, TeacherTube, and other sites that can be appropriately used in education. If community concerns suggest a high level of fear, we
advocate having administrators as active participants on all teacher social network accounts to assure that the content on the teacher's account is all educationally related and not social in
nature.

Step 6: Create Initial Content

> Rather than firewall blocks, we advocate an acceptable use policy.

Once a Facebook (or Ning
or Edmodo) page is established,
you should upload some con-
tent, and that might include a variety of items. For example, teachers should
initially write a brief paragraph on the unit under study and, if appropriate,
ask students their opinions on one of the major issues or concepts within that
unit. This initial question can often begin an exciting, in-depth discussion of
that issue or topic.

We recommend that teachers add pictures or short videos relative to the topic
under study when they can locate such pictures. In many cases, teachers seek out
short videos (try a search at YouTube or TeacherTube to find high-quality videos
that address the topic). Teachers should always preview the video or digital image
carefully prior to assigning it to the class via the Facebook page. At that point, you
can either upload the video or provide a link to it and request that students go to
that link and view the video.

One caution—do not put in too much content. While Facebook is an excellent way to heighten student interest, it is still not the most appropriate format for presenting large chunks of information or multiple videos at a time; a better format for that type of extensive assignment is a class wiki (see Tech Tool 4).

Step 7: Invite Students (and Parents) to Participate

The final step in this process is to invite students to join you on Facebook by sending a "friend" request. That process is straightforward and virtually any student who is familiar with Facebook can assist in that regard. You should make a determined effort to use Facebook to compliment students (individually or in small groups) on work they have completed successfully. Remember that parents often follow along on Facebook, and complimenting students on work well done certainly assists teachers in building successful relationships with both parents and students!

Step 8: Post Daily

Once all class members have joined you on Facebook, you should make an effort to post something to that Facebook page daily or at least every other day. These may be compliments on work, as noted above, or simple reminders of homework that is due, or quizzes that are planned for the class. You can post notes on interesting things for students to explore or make notes for students to review. Also post a sentence or two about any local or national news items that are related to class content, with a suggestion from the teacher that students follow a particular news item online. Because so many students enjoy Facebook, and participate on that site for many hours weekly, it is likely that a Facebook page for your class will dramatically increase the interest and engagement of your students (Watters, 2011).

How Do I Differentiate Using Facebook?

In classroom applications of Facebook, teachers can choose to post private comments to particular students, suggesting study strategies or particular items to consider related to the content. In that sense, social networking can foster high levels of differentiation. Further, in instances in which students are creating comments of other content for Facebook, the students' selection of tasks results in some degree of differentiation. As in many tech-tool applications, students are likely to consider their own learning-style preferences in creating content to share with the teacher or other students. Visually oriented students are more likely to share graphics, videos, and the like, whereas linguistically talented students might share comments or text. In this format, once again students tend to differentiate themselves by their selection of what they create and share with their teacher and classmates.

Conclusion

Like many tech tools, the use of Facebook fosters intensive collaboration between students, and this is quite likely to increase student engagement. In fact, it would be no stretch of imagination to place this Facebook section in the previous section of the book that focused specifically on increasing engagement and student empowerment. With that noted, there are a wide variety of social network options that can be used in education, and these represent, in some ways, the cutting edge of technology applications as this book was written in 2012. While teachers may have to jump a few hurdles related to outdated school policies and firewalls, the use of social networks to foster learning networks is well worth the time. We urge all teachers to experiment with one or more of these social networking tools as an educational option in their classroom.

References

Anderson, P. (2012). Group hopes "The Pact" inspires, brings people together: Using Facebook in schools. *The Lacrosse Tribune*. Retrieved from http://lacrossetribune.com/news/facebook-a -book-and-a-book-club–/article_8b58cc1e-6363-11e1-83b9-001871e3ce6c.html

Ferriter, B. (2011). Using Twitter in high school classrooms. Retrieved from http://teacherleaders. typepad.com/the-tempered-radical/2011/10/using-twitter-with-teens-html?utm_ source=feedburner&utm_medium=feed&utm_campaign-feed%3A+the_tempered_radical+%28 The+Tempered+Radical%29

Ferriter, W. M., & Garry, A. (2010). *Teaching the iGeneration: 5 easy ways to introduce essential skills with Web 2.0 tools*. Bloomington, IN: Solution Tree Press.

Kessler, S. (2011). *5 best practices for educators on Facebook*. Retrieved from http:// mashable.com/2011/12/05/educators-on-facebook

List, J. S., & Bryant, B. (2009). Integrating interactive online content at an early college high school: An exploration of Moodle, Ning, and Twitter. *Meridian Middle School Computer Technologies Journal, 12*(1). Retrieved from http://www.ncsu.edu/meridian/winter2009

Phillips, L. F. (2011). 5 tips for teachers to navigate Facebook's features and risks. *New York Times*. Retrieved from http://www.nytimes.com/schoolbook/2011/12/22/5-tips-for-teachers-to -navigate-facebook's-features-and-risks

Richardson, W., & Mancabelli, R. (2011). *Personal learning networks: Using the power of connections to transform education*. Bloomington, IN: Solution Tree Press.

Watters, A. (2011). *Distractions begone! Facebook as a study tool*. Retrieved from http:// mindshift.kqed.org/2011/09/distractions-set-aside-facebook-as-a-study-tool

Wilmarth, S. (2010). Five socio-technology trends that change everything in teaching and learning. In H. H. Jacobs, *Curriculum 21: Essential education for a changing world*. Alexandria, VA: ASCD.

Tech Tool 20

Twitter

What Do I Need to Know?

Another option for reaching C2S2 students is the use of *Twitter.* Twitter (www.twitter.com) is another free social networking site that can be used by educators in several ways, including classroom use. Unlike Facebook, Twitter is a microblogging service in which each posting in Twitter is specifically limited to one hundred forty characters, and it has become an excellent source for information on professional development in education. It is not intended to present oneself to the world in the way that Facebook does, but rather presents brief synopses of one's thoughts and ideas. Even with that restriction on message length, there are still many uses of Twitter in the teaching and learning process, and this site is being used by many educators today (Brumley, 2010; Ferriter, 2011). Twitter allows teachers and students to send and read brief blog-like messages, with each message focused specifically on the topic at hand. These messages are called *tweets* and are posted on the author's Twitter page, as well as on the pages of anyone following the author in his or her social network.

Twitter has been one of the fastest-growing social networks since 2008 (Richardson & Mancabelli, 2011). This stems from the fact that Twitter can be used in a wider variety of ways than Facebook, including both in class applications and professional development for teachers. Each of these is discussed below.

Definition: Twitter is a microblogging service in which each posting in Twitter is specifically limited to one hundred forty characters, and it has become an excellent source for information on professional development in education.

Twitter for Professional Development

Once a teacher or student has established a Twitter account, the user can sign up to "follow" their friends, their teacher, political candidates, various famous persons, or others. However, one important use of Twitter in education involves finding and participating in free or low-cost professional development opportunities (Brumley, 2010; "28 Creative Ways," 2011). As an example, once you establish a Twitter account, you can sign up to follow anyone on Twitter, including, for example, the senior author of this text, if you like (follow along at Twitter.com/williambender1). I use that account exclusively as a way to share information on interesting articles, brief videos, or websites that may be useful for educators, and I typically post two or three times each week. This is a good source for a variety of educational items that educators are interested in, such as notices of good teaching ideas or online education articles that might be of interest to other educators. Teachers can even use Twitter and sign up to follow tweets from professional development organizations like the Partnership for 21st Century Learning (www.p21.org).

Brumley (2010) emphasized the importance of hashtags (i.e., the symbol #) in using Twitter for professional development. A hashtag that appears prior to any term in a tweet can limit the term to specific types of content. For example, searching in Twitter for the term *apple* results in literally millions of mentions of apples in virtually any context you can imagine, whereas a search for *#apple* results in tweets limited to Apple Computers since that company uses the # to delineate content related to that specific topic. Teachers might begin exploring Twitter in their subject area by searching for #socialstudies or a similar topic. Using the #socialstudies search, you will receive ideas from educators on that topic. Of course, you might substitute science, mathematics, or other topics as you desire.

Twitter in the Classroom

Because of the desire for a social networking among today's C2S2 students, teachers have begun to use Twitter in a wide variety of ways in the classroom (Brumley, 2010; "28 Creative Ways," 2011; Ferriter, 2011). Because the length of each tweet is quite limited, this is not a place to put up lengthy assignments, content discussions, lists of readings, or digital videos. A class blog, discussed previously, would be more appropriate for those types of postings. However, teachers can use Twitter to remind students of class activities ("Remember the quiz tomorrow on the solar system! Study up!"), or teachers can highlight news stories related to class content. Teachers can also encourage parents to sign up to follow them on Twitter, and when some parents get a reminder like the one above about a class quiz, they might be prompted to remind their kids to study for that quiz.

Twitter can also be used as a classroom teaching tool to make class discussions and presentations much more interactive (Ferriter, 2011; Richardson & Mancabelli, 2011). In one example, a teacher in California required students to tweet (using laptops or smartphones) during class discussions. The teacher followed those tweets on his computer, using his Twitter account. Students were asked to tweet their thoughts, ideas, or questions during the discussion, and once those reached the teacher's computer, he could access those tweets, and send all of the tweets directly to the interactive whiteboard in the class to share with the class. Using this idea, during the class discussion itself, the teacher and all class members could see the tweets (i.e., the thoughts) of all other members of the class during that class discussion (this is similar to Wiffiti, Tech Tool 7). Further, the teacher could see who was and who was not tweeting relative to the class content, and he could then prompt those students to participate more actively. In that sense, Twitter increased the participation of all students in the class discussion. Needless to say, the students in that school considered those class discussions to be among the most interesting activities during their entire school day!

> Twitter can also be used as a classroom teaching tool to make classes much more interactive.

Other Classroom Applications for Twitter

With these examples noted, the list of possible applications is limited only by the ideas and energy of the teacher. Many sources provide specific examples, and the list below represents a compilation of classroom applications of Twitter from a variety of sources ("28 Creative Ways," 2011; Ferriter, 2011; List & Bryant, 2009; TEEContributor, 2011a, 2011b).

Request Tweets in Character. C2S2 students are used to role-playing and teachers can use that! Have students pretend to be a character under study and tweet as if they were that character. They might then explain why they tweeted in a particular way or represented a particular idea in their tweet (TEEContributor, 2011a, 2011b). As an interesting modification of this concept, teachers may require students to tweet both in character and in a specific time. For example, what tweets would General Westmorland have sent each week during January and February of 1968, while both the Battle of Khe Sanh and the Tet Offensive raged in Vietnam? What would have been Oppenheimer's tweets during the spring and summer of 1945 as the first atomic bomb was developed and ultimately tested?

TwHistory is a website where students can re-enact historical events as if they were participating, by using Twitter to communicate their thoughts as the events unfold (www.twHistory.org). Students should be encouraged to tweet in "real time" during various events (e.g., various tweets for a.m. and p.m. on each day of the three-day Battle of Gettysburg). Students will have to examine primary sources and get in character (e.g., General Mead, commander of the Union Army, or General Robert E. Lee, commanding the Confederate Army of Northern Virginia).

Use Twitter as a Backchannel for Brainstorming. Twitter is often a one-to-one communication, and teachers can use it to have students "tweet the most valuable point from class today!" Teachers can then determine whether or not to share that tweet (Ferriter, 2011). Ferriter (2011) indicates that Twitter is a more "casual" space that Facebook or other social networking sites. This probably results from the one hundred forty character limitation for tweet length. At any rate, this casual feel of Twitter seems to encourage a more open exchange of ideas.

Use Twitter to Empower Students. Several sources (Ferriter, 2011; TEEContributor, 2011a) mentioned the idea of having students tweet with local politicians, authors, or content experts, and seek answers to specific questions on various issues. While teachers have, for many decades, had students write their congressman, this new tech tool facilitates that, making the communication much easier. In that sense, Twitter can give students a voice on the local political scene much more easily than previously.

Follow Experts in Content Areas. Students should be encouraged to follow various scientists, mathematicians, or other professionals working in various areas. Having student follow scientists who may be involved in cutting-edge research on the topic under study can add an element of excitement to the instructional unit ("28 Creative Ways," 2011).

Require Foreign Language Tweets. Foreign language teachers may require students to communicate in a foreign language in a variety of ways (TEEContributor, 2011a, 2011b). Teachers may also tweet a sentence in a foreign language each day for students to interpret ("28 Creative Ways," 2011).

Conduct Classroom Polls. Using Twitter to conduct quick classroom polls can encourage student interest in the topic under study ("28 Creative Ways," 2011; TEEContributor, 2011b). In fact, this idea could easily be expanded to schoolwide polling on local or national issues.

Use Twitter for Homework Assistance. Students can use Twitter as they complete homework assignments to request assistance from other students or from the teachers ("28 Creative Ways," 2011; List & Bryant, 2009; TEEContributor, 2011a).

Tweet Notes on Sources While Conducting Research. How many millions of students (or teachers) have been frustrated by lost note cards during a research project? Loosing source material is a giant issue when doing research, and having students tweet notes on sources can eliminate that problem as well as make sources more widely available for all students (TEEContributor, 2011a).

Hold A Twitter Game Show. Teachers use game formats frequently for reviewing material, and Twitter can make that more engaging. By dividing the class into teams and providing one Internet-capable device per team, teachers can structure a game show to facilitate review prior to a class quiz (TEEContributor, 2011b).

As these examples indicate, there are many instances in which classwork and homework can be enriched by using Twitter, and teachers constantly report seeing increased student engagement with their subject as their students are invited to participate in their studies using this exciting tech tool (Ferriter, 2011; TEEContributor, 2011a, 2011b).

How Do I Get Started Using Twitter?

Step 1: Begin by Setting up a Twitter Account

To begin using Twitter, teachers should go to the Twitter website (www .twitter.com) and complete the application process. That website requires an e-mail address, and signing up for a twitter account is fully explained. Once the teacher's account is established, the teacher should determine how she wishes to use the Twitter account (receiving and sharing professional development ideas, using Twitter in the classroom, or both). Of course, teachers may wish to use Twitter for their own professional development initially, while they investigate school policies relative to using this (or any social networking site) with their students.

Step 2: Use Twitter Initially for Professional Development

The use of Twitter for professional development was described above, and this use of Twitter is not subject to any school district permissions since students would not be involved. Teachers might still run into firewall problems, but those can be sidestepped by using a personal computer at home.

Step 3: Consider the Other Social Networking Issues

If teachers choose to use Twitter in the classroom, all of the issues discussed above in the section on using Facebook in the classroom will need to be considered and addressed. In the interest of saving space (and trees!) these will not be repeated here. However, we do recommend that teachers tackle these hurdles as they arise since the benefits of using Twitter in the classroom, as shown in the examples above, far outweigh any initial trouble in overcoming these barriers, at least in most schools and school districts.

How Do I Differentiate Using Twitter?

Social networking in teaching involves a number of differentiated instructional options. For example, in the *Twitter Game Show* strategy above, teachers might group students by virtue of learning styles or preferences and then conduct the game show format, while encouraging students to address the questions using their learning-style strength. Clearly, these social networking options tap into the learning strength of interpersonal learners, those who seem to thrive and learn best when working in small groups.

Next, as the teacher follows tweets of specific students, she can often detect specific areas of misunderstanding, and these can be corrected privately. Thus, individual tweets tend to highlight individual learning needs of each student quite specifically. Finally, for students with lower motivation to participate in class, this tool is excellent. Twitter represents, in one sense, a forced interaction since teachers can easily follow who is participating and who is not, and they can direct their instructional activities or questions appropriately. In that sense, Twitter, like most social network applications in education, is likely to lead to higher student participation, even from students who would not normally complete their class or homework assignments (Wilmarth, 2010). These advantages make Twitter and other social networking options powerful teaching tools, which easily lend themselves to differentiated instruction.

Conclusions

Nothing can make a class seem more modern than the educational application of some type of social media, and Twitter certainly seems as modern as any tech tool in this book. Of course, social media can be structured within various classroom-based systems (e.g., Ning or Facebook), but Twitter is free and is certainly becoming a household term. Teachers should certainly consider using this tech tool in order to address the desires of C2S2 students for socially based learning experiences.

References

28 Creative Ways Teachers are Using Twitter. (2011). *Best Colleges Online.com*. Retrieved from http://www.bestcollegesonline.com/blog/2011/07/06/28-creative-ways-teachers-are-using-Twitter

Brumley, M. (2010). Twitter. *Teacher Experience Exchange*. Retrieved from http://h30411.www3.hp.com/discussions/68996?mcid=Twitter

Ferriter, B. (2011). *Using Twitter in high school classrooms*. Retrieved from http://teacherleaders.typepad.com/the-tempered-radical/2011/10/using-twitter-with-teens-html?utm_source=feedburner&utm_medium=feed&utm_campaign-feed%3A+the_tempered_radical+%28The+Tempered+Radical%29

List, J. S., & Bryant, B. (2009). Integrating interactive online content at an early college high school: An exploration of Moodle, Ning, and Twitter. *Meridian Middle School Computer Technologies Journal, 12*(1). Retrieved from http://www.ncsu.edu/meridian/winter2009

Richardson, W., & Mancabelli, R. (2011). *Personal learning networks: Using the power of connections to transform education*. Bloomington, IN: Solution Tree Press.

TEEContributor. (2011a). *5 ways to use Twitter in the classroom*. Retrieved from http://h30411.www3.hp.com/posts/1014985-5_ways_to_use_Twitter_in_the_classroom

TEEContributor. (2011b). *5 more ways to use Twitter in the classroom*. Retrieved from http://h30411.www3.hp.com/posts/1118287-Five_more_ways_to_use-Twitter_in_the_classroom?mcid=Twitter

Wilmarth, S. (2010). Five socio-technology trends that change everything in teaching and learning. In H. H. Jacobs, *Curriculum 21: Essential education for a changing world*. Alexandria, VA: ASCD.

Part V

The Teaching Revolution and a Brave New World for the 21st Century

We believe that this book will help many teachers as they begin their journey into 21st century teaching. While we have described twenty options that we are confident most teachers can learn and begin to use with relative ease, there are literally hundreds (if not thousands) of other tech tools that could have been described herein. Our main selection criteria involved presenting relatively user-friendly tech tools that were being used fairly widely in classrooms today, and are generally under the control of the teacher rather than the school or school district.

As we've indicated throughout this book, rather than implementation of specific tech tools, it is critical that all teachers understand, in

Rather than implementation of specific tech tools, it is critical that all teachers understand, in a broader sense, how the teaching and learning process is changing today.

a broader sense, how the teaching and learning process is changing today given this massive influx of technology into the 21st century classroom. In fact, the teaching-learning process is undergoing a fundamental revolution, a revolution in technique and practices that has been described previously as representing the interface of differentiated instruction, instructional pedagogy, and technology (Bender & Waller, 2011; Richardson, 2012; Waters, 2011). Educators have noted that students today learn and function within the school environment in different ways than previously, and teachers are struggling to keep up (Richardson, 2012; Waters, 2011).

The Teaching Revolution

Here is a straightforward, if somewhat embarrassing, example that might help clarify what we mean by the teaching revolution (Bender & Waller, 2011). The senior author of this text went to school, and taught in public schools, in the days prior to computer usage in the classroom. In those distant days (perhaps thirty years ago, and much less in some school districts), only three avenues existed for the delivery of new instruction to students: teacher talk, textbooks, and encyclopedias. In those days, teacher lectures, teacher-led discussion talk, and textbooks were the primary avenues for delivery of information, and occasionally, students were marched down to the library (FYI: it was a library then, rather than a media center) to use an encyclopedia. Those three teaching tools were all that was available.

In contrast, the 21st century classroom rarely, if ever, employs those traditional tools. Texts have become (or will soon become) e-books, complete with many videos embedded, links to additional information, and various adaptive reading supports (Waters, 2011). With the announcement of e-books from Apple computer in 2012, one can only wonder how long traditional, hardcopy texts will even be available. Further teacher talk (i.e., lectures, teacher-led class discussions) has given way to teacher-facilitated instruction, and with today's students, teacher talk really doesn't work anymore, unless it is supported by a broad array of tech applications (e.g., interactive whiteboards, web links, and Internet access during presentations). Clearly, teachers today must exercise 21st century tech tools as described herein, in order to remain current as a teacher of 21st century students.

We recently heard a proponent of technology in the classroom make a very extreme statement to a small group of educators. While we disagree with this somewhat, it is still an interesting position for teachers to consider.

If you're talking while teaching content to the whole class at once, you're probably doing it wrong!

Embedded within that statement is the fundamental shift in teaching from teacher talk to teacher-facilitated learning. Further, while we don't agree entirely with this sentiment, it is correct insofar as the teacher-talk method of content delivery never really worked for all of the students in the class, though it may have worked

> If you're talking while teaching content to the whole class at once, you're probably doing it wrong!

for students in the middle range of academic achievement. Traditionally the teacher-talk method of teaching does not offer many options for differentiating instruction, and thus, the wide variety of instructional needs were simply not adequately addressed.

Another reason we often refer to this statement is it places the tech revolution in the context of appropriate pedagogy for instruction. It is not that technology itself will transform learning; rather, technology in the context of highly differentiated instruction is likely to have the positive benefits we seek for our students. As discussed in the introduction of this book, "the box is not enough!" Tech-based teaching must be placed within sound instructional principles, such as provision of highly differentiated instruction targeted to individual student needs, as well as student-centered, student-generated projects, in order to realize the maximum benefits for our students (Bender & Waller, 2011).

C2S2 Kids and the Learning Revolution

We have shown throughout this book that students today prefer to learn in a manner different from students only a decade ago. These C2S2 students set high expectations for today's teachers, and designing instructional activities consistent with those needs is one of the most important tasks teachers have to undertake. In fact, those four C2S2 expectations—collaborative instruction, creativity, social learning, and self-directed learning—are singularly the most important driving force in 21st century classrooms, and educators ignore that fact at their peril. In other contexts, this has been referred to as "teaching the iGeneration," or "personalized learning," but we prefer our C2S2 synthesis of these learning characteristics and expectations. What all would agree on is the fact that the learner has changed, and teachers must address that change; in that sense, a Learning Revolution has indeed paralleled the Teaching Revolution, and both have already begun (Bender & Waller, 2011).

What Do I Do Now?

For lower-tech teachers, and again, we believe that accurately represents all teachers, we believe that this book is an excellent beginning. The next steps involve only three very specific goals.

Goal 1: Use the Four Critical Tech Tools. We've identified four tech tools in the first section for all teachers to implement immediately, if they have not already done so. These included:

- *Ensure Internet access in some fashion* (and it may be as basic as making multiday assignments for students to complete using a BYOD plan)
- *Design and use webquests*
- *Begin blogging*
- *Set up a class wiki*

> Teachers should set a specific goal—One month from now, I will be teaching with these four tools and ideas!

These can be accomplished within a few weeks after reading this book. Again, seek guidance and help from other teachers within the school or the school district technology person and set a specific goal—One month from now, I will be teaching with these four tools and ideas!

> Set a second goal—Two months from now, I will be using a social networking site personally and if possible, in my teaching.

Goal Two: Socialize the Learning! After teachers have implemented those four tech tools, we would add a social-learning element. We suggest using Twitter initially, because, even if the school or district has policies against use of social networks in teaching, a personal Twitter account should be set up by every teacher for professional development ideas. Also while school policies in some districts do prohibit use of some of these sites, more restricted social networking sites or even class e-mail options would help socialize the learning process for the students. Thus we recommend this second goal—Two months from now, I will be using a social networking site personally and if possible, in my teaching.

Goal Three: Foster Collaborative Learning! Collaborative learning is not only an option for teaching; it is an absolute expectation in the 21st century workplace. Teachers must implement tech tools that foster collaboration, and here we would recommend two: use either Google Apps or Scribd. While both of these tech tools offer collaborative publishing opportunities, Google Apps, simply because of the size of that company, might be exactly the tech tool that today's students use in the workplace in 2020 or 2025. Thus, we recommend a third goal—Three months from now, I will be using Google Apps or another student publishing tool in teaching.

> Set a third goal—Three months from now, I will be using Google Apps or another student publishing tool in teaching.

We should note that we have not recommended a specific goal on use of self-directed curriculum, such as Khan Academy. To put the matter bluntly, such curricula simply don't exist in every subject area. However, for all teachers in mathematics, we would highly recommend that they implement self-directed learning using Khan Academy in their math programs. For many students, this can be the key to unlock amazing potential.

If every teacher would undertake these three goals, the teaching-learning process would be absolutely transformed, and the amazing creative powers of students worldwide would be unleashed. And that leads into a very interesting future.

C2S2 Adults and Our Future!

In closing, we might well ask what types of learners—fundamentally, what types of adults—do we wish to foster or create in our classrooms? Richardson (2012) recently suggested an interesting thought—perhaps we might seek to prepare students to learn without us! Students might be taught to master content without any dependence on teachers, using technology options that are only now becoming available. Students will become more self-directed and will exercise much more influence over what they learn and when they learn.

This might ultimately lead to a sort of personalized learning, one that reaches beyond differentiated instruction to the point at which instruction is delivered individually, based on highly targeted, highly specific needs of individual students (Richardson, 2012). In some ways, the recent response-to-intervention initiative exemplifies personalized learning. In that context, these authors recently argued that response-to-intervention differentiated instruction and technology will, working in a symbiotic relationship, revolutionize the teaching-learning process, and again, this places technology squarely in the context of sound instructional pedagogy (Bender & Waller, 2011).

What does seem clear is that learners of today, as citizens of tomorrow, will need to be C2S2 adults; they will need to be collaborative, creative, social, and self-directed learners. They must be adults who can learn and master content on their own (see Tech Tool 6—Khan Academy, as one early example), and they will use tech resources to do that. Further, they must function well in collaborative tasks, which are exactly the types of tasks they seem to enjoy. Thus, we want to facilitate the growth of (here, please note that we refuse to use the 19th century view represented by the term *produce*) a self-directed, independent learner who can successfully collaborate with peers in solving real-world problems. Clearly technology will play a very significant role in that, but technology is only a set of tools—it is not the underlying framework for either learning or for accomplishing tasks in the adult world. Rather, technology must be implemented in service to sound, tried-and-true instructional principals—scaffolded instruction and differentiated instruction, to name but two.

Thus, we recommend what we believe to be the most worthy goal for every educator today. Our educational goal should be nothing less than the creation of C2S2 learners for the 21st century, empowered with every tech tool available, who focus on relevant, significant problems and seek 21st century solutions. Therein lies the future of the teaching-learning process, if not (in some lofty sense) the very future of our schools and perhaps of our species.

Once again we say to all who feel or have felt the call to become 21st century educators—begin now and enjoy the journey!

> Our educational goal should be nothing less than the creation of independent, self-directed 21st century learners, empowered with every tech tool available, who focus on relevant, significant problems and seek 21st century solutions.

References

Bender, W. N., & Waller, L. (2011). *The teaching revolution: RTI, technology, and differentiation transform teaching for the 21st Century.* Thousand Oaks, CA: Corwin.

Richardson, W. (2012). Preparing students to learn without us. *Educational Leadership, 69*(5), 22–26. Retrieved from http://www.ascd.org/publications/educationa-leadership/feb12/vol69/num05/Preparing-Students-to-Learn-Without-Us.aspx

Waters, J. K. (2011). Broadband, social networks, and mobility have spawned a new kind of learner. *THE Journal.* Retrieved from http://thejournal.com/Articles/2011/12/13/Broadband-Social-Networks-and-Mobility.aspx?Page=1

Index

Note: In page references, f indicates figures.

CORWIN
A SAGE Company

The Corwin logo—a raven striding across an open book—represents the union of courage and learning. Corwin is committed to improving education for all learners by publishing books and other professional development resources for those serving the field of PreK–12 education. By providing practical, hands-on materials, Corwin continues to carry out the promise of its motto: **"Helping Educators Do Their Work Better."**

DATE DUE